AN EXPLORER'S ADVENTURES

IN TIBET

AN EXPLORER'S ADVENTURES

IN TIBET

A. HENRY SAVAGE LANDOR

GYAN

Published by

Gyan Publishing House
5, Ansari Road
Daryaganj, New Delhi-110002
Phone: 011-47034999, 9811692060
E-mail: books@gyanbooks.com

Distribution Network
gyanbooks.com
India, USA, Canada, UK, Australia, France

ISBN: 978-81-212-9380-8 (PB)
First Published, 1910

2nd Impression 2023

Printed at: Gyan Press, Delhi.

AN EXPLORER'S ADVENTURES IN TIBET

AUTHOR: A. HENRY SAVAGE LANDOR

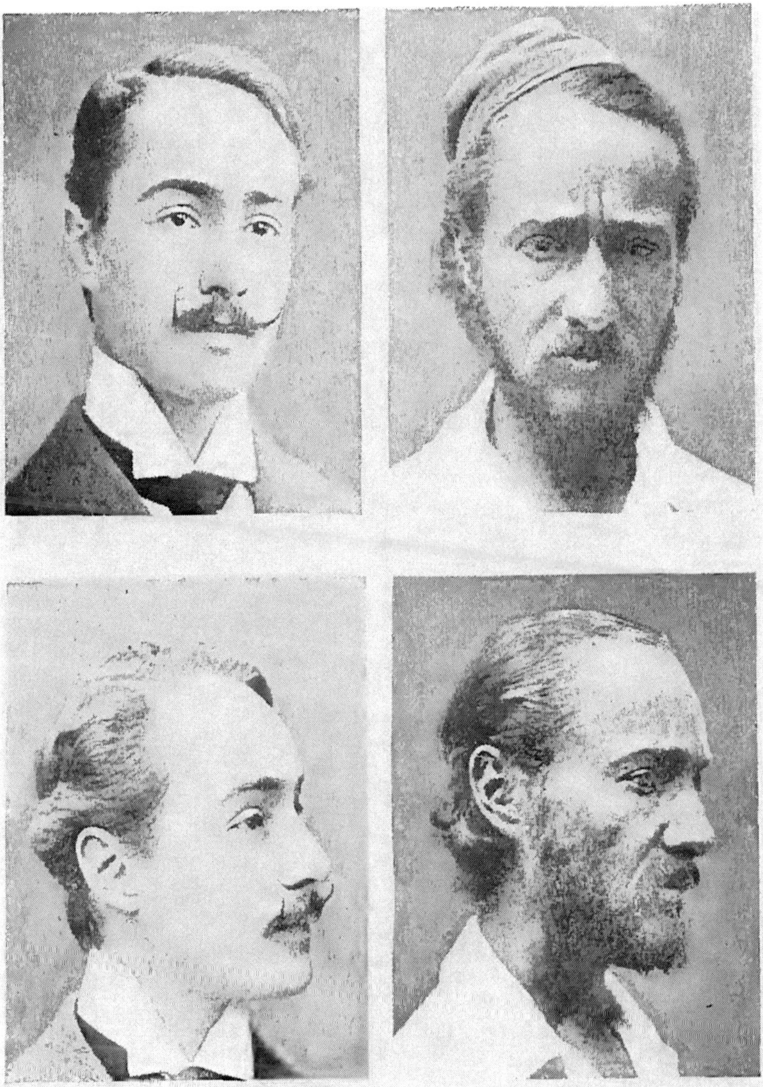

THE AUTHOR, FEBRUARY, 1897 THE AUTHOR, OCTOBER, 1897

AN EXPLORER'S ADVENTURES
IN TIBET

BY

A. HENRY SAVAGE LANDOR

AUTHOR OF
"IN THE FORBIDDEN LAND"
"THE GEMS OF THE EAST"
ETC. ETC.

WITH ILLUSTRATIONS
BY THE AUTHOR

HARPER & BROTHERS PUBLISHERS
NEW YORK AND LONDON
MCMX

CONTENTS

ILLUSTRATIONS

PREFACE

THIS book deals chiefly with the author's adventures during a journey taken in Tibet in 1897, when that country, owing to religious fanaticism, was closed to strangers. For the scientific results of the expedition, for the detailed description of the customs, manners, etc., of the people, the larger work, entitled *In the Forbidden Land* (Harper & Brothers, publishers), by the same author, should be consulted.

During that journey of exploration the author made many important geographical discoveries, among which may be mentioned:

(*a*) The discovery of the two principal sources of the Great Brahmaputra River, one of the four largest rivers in the world.

(*b*) The ascertaining that a high range of mountains existed north of the Himahlyas, but with no such great elevations as the highest of the Himahlyan range.

(*c*) The settlement of the geographical controversy regarding the supposed connection between the Sacred (Mansarowar) and the Devil's (Rakastal) lakes.

(*d*) The discovery of the real sources of the Sutlej River.

In writing geographical names the author has given

the names their true sounds as locally pronounced, and has made no exception even for the poetic word "Him-ahlya" (the abode of snow), which in English is usually misspelt and distorted into the meaningless Himalaya.

All bearings of the compass given in this book are magnetic. Temperature observations were registered with Fahrenheit thermometers.

A. H. S. L.

AN EXPLORER'S ADVENTURES IN TIBET

AN EXPLORER'S ADVENTURES IN TIBET

CHAPTER I

A FORBIDDEN COUNTRY

TIBET was a forbidden land. That is why I went there. This strange country, cold and barren, lies on a high tableland in the heart of Asia. The average height of this desolate tableland—some 15,000 feet above sea-level—is higher than the highest mountains of Europe. People are right when they call it the "roof of the world." Nothing, or next to nothing, grows on that high plateau, except poor shrubs and grass in the lower valleys. The natives live on food imported from neighboring countries. They obtain this by giving in exchange wool, borax, iron, and gold.

High mountain ranges bound the Tibetan plateau on all sides. The highest is the Himahlya range to the south, the loftiest mountain range on earth. From the south it is only possible to enter Tibet with an expedition in summer, when the mountain passes are not entirely blocked by snow.

At the time of my visit the law of Tibet was that no stranger should be allowed to enter the country. The Tibetan frontier was closely guarded by soldiers.

A few expeditions had travelled in the northern part of Tibet, as the country was there practically uninhabited. They had met with no one to oppose their march save, perhaps, a few miserable nomads. No one, since Tibet became a forbidden country to strangers, had been able to penetrate in the Province of Lhassa—the only province of Tibet with a comparatively thick population. It was this province, the most forbidden of all that forbidden land, that I intended to explore and survey. I succeeded in my object, although I came very near paying with my life for my wish to be of use to science and my fellow-creatures.

With the best equipment that money could buy for scientific work, I started for the Tibetan frontier in 1897. From Bombay, in India, I travelled north to the end of the railway, at Kathgodam, and then by carts and horses to Naini Tal. At this little hill-station on the lower Himahlyas, in the north-west Province of India, I prepared my expedition, resolved to force my way in the Unknown Land.

Naini Tal is 6407 feet above the level of the sea. From this point all my loads had to be carried on the backs of coolies or porters. Therefore, each load must not exceed fifty pounds in weight. I packed instruments, negatives, and articles liable to get damaged in cases of my own manufacture, specially designed for rough usage. A set of four such cases of well-seasoned deal wood, carefully joined and fitted, zinc-lined and soaked in a special preparation by which they were rendered water and air tight, could be made useful in many ways. Taken separately, they could be used as seats. Four placed in a row, answered the purpose of a bedstead. Three could be used as seat and table. The combination of four, used in a certain manner, made a punt, or boat, of quick, solid, and easy construction, with which an unfordable river could be crossed, or for taking soundings in the still waters of unexplored lakes. The cases could be used as tanks for photographic work. In case of emergency they might serve even as water-casks for carrying water in regions where it was not to be found. Each of these boxes, packed, was exactly a coolie load, or else in sets of two they could be slung over a pack-saddle by means of straps with rings.

My provisions had been specially prepared for me, and were suited to the severe climate and the high elevations I should find myself in. The preserved meats contained a vast amount of fat and carbonaceous, or heat-making food, as well as elements easily digestible and calculated to maintain one's strength in moments of unusual stress. I carried a .256 Mannlicher rifle, a Martini-Henry, and 1000 cartridges duly packed in a water-tight case. I also had a revolver with 500 cartridges, a number of hunting-knives, skinning implements, wire traps of several sizes for capturing small mammals, butterfly-nets, bottles for preserving reptiles in alcohol, insect-killing bottles (cyanide of potassium), a quantity of arsenical soap, bone nippers, scalpels, and all other accessories necessary for the collection of natural-history specimens. There were in my outfit three sets of photographic cameras, and 158 dozen dry plates, as well as all adjuncts for the developing, fixing, printing, etc., of the negatives. I had two complete sets of instruments for astronomical observations and for use in surveying. One set had been given to me by the Royal Geographical Society of London. The other was my own. Each set consisted of the following instruments. A six-inch sextant. The hypsometrical apparatus, a device used for measuring heights by means of boiling-point thermometers, which had been specially constructed for work at great elevations. It is well known that the higher one goes, the lower is the temperature at which water boils. By measuring the temperature of boiling water and at the same time the temperature of the atmosphere at any high point on a mountain, and working out a computation in relation to the boiling-point temperature of a given place on the sea-level, one can obtain with accuracy the difference in height between the two points.

Two aneroid barometers were also carried, which were specially made for me—one registering heights to 20,000 feet, the other to 25,000 feet. Although I used these aneroids principally for differential heights along my route, as aneroids cannot always be relied upon for great accuracy, I found on checking these particular instruments with the boiling-point thermometers that they were always extremely accurate. This was, however, exceptional, and it would not do for any one to rely on aneroids alone for the exact measurement of mountain heights. There were in my outfit three artificial horizons—one with mercury, the others constructed with a plate glass. The latter had a special arrangement by which they could be levelled to a nicety. I found that for taking observations for latitude and longitude by the sun the mercury horizon was satisfactory, but when occultations had to be taken at night the plate-glass horizons were easier to work, and gave a more clearly defined reflection of stars and planets in such a bitterly cold climate as Tibet, where astronomical observations were always taken under great difficulty. The most useful instrument I carried on that expedition was a powerful telescope with astronomical eyepiece. Necessarily, I carried a great many compasses, which included prismatic, luminous, floating, and pocket compasses. Maximum and minimum thermometers were taken along to keep a record of the daily temperature, and I also took with me a box of drawing and painting materials, as well as all kinds of instruments for map-making, such as protractors, parallel rules, tape rules, section paper, note-books, etc. I had water-tight half-chronometer watches keeping Greenwich mean time, and three other watches. In order to work out on the spot my observations for latitude and longitude, I had with me such books as *Raper's Navigation* and the *Nautical Almanac* for the years 1897 and 1898, in which all the necessary tables for the computations were to be found.

I was provided with a light mountain tent, usually called a *tente d'abri*; it was seven feet long, four feet wide, and three feet high; it weighed four pounds. All

I needed in the way of bedding was one camel's-hair blanket. My clothing was reduced to a minimum. My head-gear was a mere straw hat, which was unfortunately destroyed at the beginning of my journey, so that I went most of the time with my head uncovered or else wore a small cap. I wore medium thick shoes without nails, and never carried a stick. It was largely due to the simplicity of my personal equipment that I was able to travel with great speed often under trying circumstances. Although the preparations for my expedition cost me several thousand dollars, I spent little money on medicines for myself and my men; in fact, all they cost me was sixty-two cents (two shillings and sixpence). I am firm in the belief that any healthy man living naturally under natural conditions, and giving himself plenty of exercise, can be helped very little by drugs.

I started from Naini Tal and rode to Almora (5510 feet above sea-level), the last hill-station toward the Tibetan frontier where I expected to find European residents. At this place I endeavored to obtain plucky, honest, wiry, healthy servants who would be ready, for the sake of a good salary and a handsome reward, to brave the many discomforts, hardships, and perils my expedition into Tibet was likely to involve. Scores of servants presented themselves. Each one produced a certificate with praises unbounded of all possible virtues that a servant could possess. Each certificate was duly ornamented with the signature of some Anglo-Indian officer — either a governor, a general, a captain, or a deputy commissioner. What struck me mostly was that bearers of these testimonials seemed sadly neglected by those who had been so enthusiastically pleased with their services. They all began by begging, or else asked, for a loan of rupees in order to buy food, clothes, and support the dear ones they would be leaving behind.

I was sitting one day in the post resting-house when an odd creature came to offer his services. "Where are your certificates?" I asked.

"*Sahib, hum 'certificates' ne hai*" (Sir, I have no certificates).

I employed him at once. His facial lines showed much more character than I had noticed in the features of other local natives. That was quite sufficient for me. I am a great believer in physiognomy and first impressions, which are to me more than any certificate in the world. I have so far never been mistaken.

My new servant's dress was peculiar. His head was wrapped in a white turban. From under a short waistcoat there appeared a gaudy yellow and black flannel shirt, which hung outside his trousers instead of being tucked in them. He had no shoes, and carried in his right hand an old cricket-stump, with which he "presented arms" every time I came in or went out of the room. His name was Chanden Sing. He was not a skilful valet. For instance, one day I found him polishing my shoes with my best hair-brushes. When opening soda-water bottles he generally managed to give you a spray bath, and invariably hit you in the face with the flying cork. It was owing to one of these accidents that Chanden Sing, having hurt my eye badly, was one day flung bodily out of the door. Later—as I had no more soda water left—I forgave him, and allowed him to return. It was this man who turned out to be the one plucky man among all my followers. It was he who stood by me through thick and thin during our trials in Tibet.

From Almora up to what is usually called Bhot (the country upon the Himahlya slopes on the British side of the frontier) our journey was through fairly well-known districts; therefore, I shall not dwell on the first portion of our route. I had some thirty carriers with me. We proceeded up and down, through thick forests of pine and fir trees, on the sides of successive mountain ranges.

We went through the ancient Gourkha town of Pithoragarh, with its old fort. Several days later I visited the old Rajah of Askote, one of the finest princes Northern India then possessed. I went to see the Raots, a strange race of savages living, secluded from everybody, in the forest. In a work called *In the Forbidden Land* a detailed description will be found of my experiences with those strange people, and also of our long marches through that beautiful region of the lower Himahlyas.

We reached at last a troublesome part of the journey—a place called the Nerpani, which, translated, means "the waterless trail." Few travellers had been as far as this point. I shall not speak of the ups and down at precipitous angles which we found upon the trail, which had been cut along the almost vertical cliff. Here and there were many sections of the trail which were built on crowbars thrust horizontally into the rock. A narrow path had been made by laying over these crowbars large slabs of stone not particularly firm when you trod over them. As you went along this shaky path on the side of the precipice the drop down to the river at the bottom of the cliff was often from 1800 to 2000 feet, and the path in many places not wider than six inches. In other places the Nerpani trail consisted of badly put together flights of hundreds of steps along the face of the cliff.

CHAPTER II

AN UNKNOWN PASS

It was at a place called Garbyang, close to the Tibetan boundary, that I made my last preparations for my expedition into Tibet. A delay at this place was inevitable, as all the passes over the Himahlya range were closed. Fresh snow was falling daily. I intended to cross over by the Lippu Pass, the lowest of all in that region; but having sent men to reconnoitre, I found it was impossible at that time to take up my entire expedition, even by that easier way.

I had a Tibetan tent made in Garbyang. Dr. H. Wilson, of the Methodist Evangelical Mission, whom I met at this place, went to much trouble in trying to get together men for me who would accompany me over the Tibetan border. His efforts were not crowned with success. The thirty men I had taken from India refused to come any further, and I was compelled to get fresh men from this place. The Shokas (the local and correct name of the inhabitants of Bhot) were not at all inclined to accompany me. They knew too well how cruel the Tibetans were. Many of them had been tortured, and men could be seen in Garbyang who had been mutilated by the Tibetans. Indeed, the Tibetans often crossed the border to come and claim dues and taxes and inflict

INVOLUNTARY TOBOGGANING

punishment on the helpless Shokas, who were left unprotected by the Government of India.

The Jong Pen of Taklakot, a high official at the Tibetan frontier, upon hearing of my proposed visit, sent threats that he would confiscate the land of any man who came in my employ. He sent messengers threatening to cut off my head if I crossed the boundary, and promised to flog and kill any man who accompanied me. On my side I had spies keeping me well informed of his movements. He kept on sending daily messengers with more threats. He gathered his soldiers on the Lippu Pass, where he suspected I might enter his country.

Before starting with my entire expedition I took a reconnoitring trip with only a few men, in order to see what tactics I should adopt in order to dodge the fanatical natives of the forbidden land. To go and find new ways on virgin mountains and glaciers was not easy work. During our rapid scouting journey we had a number of accidents. Going over a snow-slope one day I slipped and shot down a snow-slope with terrific speed for a distance of three hundred yards, just escaping getting smashed to pieces at the end of this involuntary tobogganning. One of my carriers, who carried a child on the top of one of my loads, had a similar accident, with the result that the child was killed.

On returning to Garbyang I found that the Tibetans had tried to set the natives against me. Tibetan spies travelled daily between Taklakot and Garbyang, in order to keep the Jong Pen informed of my movements. The Jong Pen sent an impudent messenger one day to say that he had plenty of soldiers guarding the Lippu Pass, and that he would kill us all if we came. If he caught me alive he would cut off my head; my body, he said, he would sew in skins and fling into the river. I sent a messenger back to the Jong Pen to inform him that I was ready to start, and that I would meet him on the Lippu Pass; that he had better beware, and get out of my way. The messenger who brought him this news barely escaped with his life. He returned to me, saying that the Jong Pen was preparing for war, that he had gathered all his soldiers on the top of a narrow pass, where they had piled up a great number of large rocks and smaller ammunition to be rolled down upon us when we should be coming up the mountain-side.

Having collected men enough, after much trouble, I one day unexpectedly mustered them, and that same night made a sudden start. The Tibetans, suspecting that I might be leaving that day, cut down the bridge over a rapid and deep torrent forming the boundary between India and Nepal. This inconvenienced me, as I had to find my way on our side of the stream, which was very rugged. This gave us additional trouble. Some of the precipices we had to cross were extremely dangerous.

I reached the highest village in the Himahlyas, a place called Kuti, at an elevation of 12,920 feet. Here I hastily made my final preparations for the last dash across the frontier. Every available Shoka had joined my party, and no inducement brought more volunteers. I needed two extra men. Two stray shepherds turned up half famished and naked, with long, unkempt heads of hair, and merely a coral necklace and a silver bangle by way of clothing. With these two men my little force was brought up to thirty strong.

One of the two shepherds interested me. He was sulky. He seldom uttered a word, and when he did, he never spoke pleasantly. He looked painfully ill. Motionless, he would sometimes stare at a fixed point as if in a trance. His features were peculiarly refined and regular, but his skin had the ghastly, shiny, whitish tinge peculiar to lepers. I paid no special attention to him at first, as I was busy with other matters; but one day while on the march I examined him carefully, and discovered that the poor fellow had indeed all the symptoms of that most terrible of all diseases, leprosy. His distorted and contracted fingers, with the skin sore at the joints, were a sad and certain proof. I examined his feet, and found further evidence that the man was a leper.

"What is your name?" I inquired of him.

"Mansing," he said, dryly, becoming immediately again absorbed in one of his dreamy trances.

In looking over my followers I was amused to see what a strange mixture they were. There were Humlis and Jumlis, mountain tribesmen living near the Tibetan border; they wore their long black hair tied into small braids and a topknot. There were Tibetans, Shokas, Rongbas, Nepalese—all good mountaineers. Then there were Chanden Sing and Mansing belonging to the Rajiput caste. There were a Brahmin, two native Christians, and a Johari. Then Doctor Wilson. What a collection! What a confusion of languages and dialects!

An amusing feature of this odd crowd was that each particular caste looked down upon all the others. This, from the beginning, occasioned a good deal of trouble among my men. I was glad of this, as it seemed a sort of guarantee that they would never combine against me. One of the most peculiar men I had with me was a Tibetan brigand, a man with the strength of an ox. His history did not bear a close examination. He had killed many people. He asked to be employed by me, as he had quarrelled with his wife, and refused to live with her any longer. In camp he went by the name of *Daku* (the brigand). The son of one of the richest traders of Garbyang, a young fellow called Kachi, also accompanied me. He was intelligent, and could speak a few words of English. I had employed him to look after the men and to act as interpreter, if necessary. His uncle Dola was employed in the capacity of valet and cook.

Instead of proceeding by the Lippu Pass, where the Jong Pen was waiting for me with his men, I made forced marches from Kuti in a different direction altogether. I meant to cross over by a high untrodden pass, practically unknown, where no one could suspect that a caravan would enter Tibet. My men were good. We marched steadily for several days over very rough country, getting higher and higher toward the eternal snows. We suffered considerably in crossing the rapid and foaming torrents. They were often quite deep, and the water was so cold from the melting snows that we were nearly frozen each time we waded through them. We crossed several large flat basins of stones and gravel which appeared to have been lake-beds. In these basins we found deltas, formed by the stream dividing in various directions. We suffered tortures in crossing barefooted one cold stream after another. Some of my men narrowly escaped frost-bites, and it was only after rubbing their feet violently that the intense pain ceased and circulation was at last restored. The soles of my feet and my toes were badly cut and bruised. Every stone in the streams seemed to have a sharp edge. I, too, suffered agony after I had been in the water for some time. Never until that day did I know what a great comfort it was to possess a pair of warm socks! The last basin we crossed was at an elevation of 15,400 feet. We made our camp there. The thermometer registered a minimum temperature of 24°, whereas the maximum temperature that day was 51° Fahrenheit.

One of the main drawbacks of travelling at great elevations was the want of fuel. There was not a tree, not a shrub, to be seen near our camp. Nature wore her most desolate and barren look. Failing wood, my men dispersed to collect and bring in the dry dung of yaks, ponies, and sheep to serve as fuel. Kindling this was no easy matter. Box after box of matches was quickly used, and our collective lung-power severely drawn upon in blowing the unwilling sparks into a flame a few inches high. Upon this meagre fire we attempted to cook our food and boil our water (a trying process at great elevations). The cuisine that night was not of the usual excellence. We had to eat everything half-cooked, or, to be accurate, practically uncooked. The night was a bitterly cold one, and snow was falling heavily. When we rose in the morning snow was two feet deep around us. The glare was painful to our eyes. I mustered my men. Mansing was missing. He had not arrived the previous night, and there was no sign of the man I had sent in search of him. I was anxious not only for the man, but for the load he carried—a load of flour, salt, pepper, and five pounds of butter. I feared that the poor leper had been washed away in one of the dangerous streams. He must, at any rate, be suffering terribly from the cold, with no shelter and no fire.

It was long after sunrise when, with the aid of my telescope, I discovered the rescued man and rescuer coming toward us. They arrived in camp an hour or so later. Mansing had been found sound asleep, several miles back, lying flat by the side of the empty butter-pot. He had eaten all the butter. When we discovered this every one in camp was angry. The natives valued fat and butter as helping to keep them warm when going over those cold passes. With much trouble I rescued Mansing from the clutches of my other men, who wanted to punish the poor leper severely. In order that this might not happen again, I ordered Mansing to carry a heavy load of photographic plates and instruments, which I thought would not prove quite so appetizing.

While we were camping a flock of some six hundred sheep appeared, and with them some Tibetans. As I had pitched my Tibetan tent, they made for it, expecting to find some of their own countrymen. Their confusion was amusing when they found themselves face to face with Doctor Wilson and myself. Hurriedly removing their fur caps, they laid them upon the ground and made a comical bow. They put out their tongues full length, and kept them so until I made signs that they could draw them back, as I wanted them to answer several questions. This unexpected meeting with us frightened them greatly. They were trembling all over with fear. After getting as much information as they seemed to have, I bought their fattest sheep. When the money was paid there was a further display of furred tongues, and more grand salaams when they departed, while all hands in my camp were busy trying to prevent our newly purchased animals from rejoining the flock moving away from us. On our next march these animals were a great trouble. We had to drag them most of the way. Kachi, who had been intrusted with a stubborn, strong beast, which I had specially promised my men for their dinner if they made a long march that day, was outwitted by the sheep. It freed its head from the cord with which Kachi was dragging it, and cantered away full speed in the opposite direction to the one in which we were travelling. It is well known that at great altitudes running is a painful operation, for the rarefied air makes such exertion almost suffocating. Yet Kachi, having overcome his first surprise, was soon chasing the escaped beast, and, urged by the cheers of my other men, succeeded, after an exciting race, in catching the animal by its tail. This feat is easier to describe than to accomplish, for Tibetan sheep have very short, stumpy tails. Kachi fell to the ground exhausted, but he held fast with both hands to his capture, and finally the animal was secured with ropes.

Climbing over rolling ground, we rose to a pass 15,580 feet high—over a thousand feet higher than Pike's Peak, in Colorado. Then crossing a wide, flat land, we followed the Kuti River, with its high, snowy mountains to the west and east. The line of perpetual snow was at 16,000 feet; the snow below this level melted daily, except in a few shaded places. Red and white flowers were still to be seen, though not in such quantities as lower down. We saw many pairs of small butterflies with black-and-white wings.

After a while there was yet another bitterly cold stream to ford, two small lakes to skirt, and three more deep rivers to wade, with cold water from the snows reaching up to our chests. We had to make the best way we could through a large field of iron-bearing rock, which so affected my compass that for the time it became quite unreliable, owing to its deviation.

Mile after mile we marched over sharp stones, wading through another troublesome delta fully a mile in width with eight streams, and crossing a flat basin of pointed pebbles. At last, to our great comfort, we came to smooth grass-land.

Here the Kuti River flowed through a large basin, not unlike the one near which we had camped the night before. It looked like the bed of a lake, with high vertical rocks on the left. As we went on to the north-west the basin became wider and the Kuti River turned to the north-west, while the Mangshan River, descending from the east, joined the first stream in the centre of the basin. In wading through the numerous branches of the two rivers we felt more than ever the trials and weariness of the day before. The water seemed colder than ever. Our feet were by this time in a dreadful condition, bleeding and sore, because it was constantly necessary to walk barefooted rather than keep removing our foot-gear every few minutes. Aching and chilled, we stumbled on, in and out of the water, always treading, it seemed, on sharply pointed stones. The pain had to be borne patiently. At last we reached our camping-ground, situated under the lee of the high chain of mountains to the north of us and on the northern bank of the Mangshan River. Directly in front of us stood the final obstacle—the great backbone of the Himahlyas. Once across this range, I should be on the high Tibetan plateau so accurately described as "the roof of the world."

CHAPTER III

A NARROW ESCAPE

FROM Kuti I had sent a sturdy Shoka named Nattoo to find out whether it was possible to cross the Himahlyan chain over the high Mangshan Pass. In case of a favorable report, I should be able to get several marches into Tibet without fear of being detected. I reckoned on turning the position occupied by the force of soldiers which I was informed the Jong Pen of Taklakot had gathered on the Lippu Pass in order to prevent my entering his country. Before the Tibetans could have time to find where I was, I should be too far into the forbidden land for them to catch me up. Nattoo duly returned. He had been half-way up the mountain. The snow was deep, and there were huge and treacherous cracks in the ice. An avalanche had fallen, and it was merely by a miracle that he had escaped with his life. He had turned back without reaching the summit of the pass. He was scared and worn out, and declared it was impossible for us to proceed that way. The thrilling account of the Kutial's misfortunes discouraged my men. What with the intense cold, the fatigue of carrying heavy loads at high elevations over such rough country, and the dreaded icy-cold rivers which they had crossed so often, my carriers became absolutely demoralized at the thought of new hardships ahead. I did not believe Nattoo. I determined to go and see for myself.

It was half-past four in the afternoon, and therefore some little time before sunset. There should be moonlight. I had on that day marched eight miles. It must be remembered that at high elevations the effort of walking eight miles would be as great as to walk twice as far at lower altitudes. Though my feet were wounded and sore, I was not tired. Our camp was at a height of 16,150 feet, an elevation higher than the highest mountain in Europe. Doctor Wilson insisted on accompanying me on my reconnoitring trip. Kachi Ram and a Rongba coolie also volunteered to come. Bijesing, the Johari, after some persuasion, got on his feet to accompany our little exploration party. Chanden Sing was left in charge of the camp, with strict orders to punish severely any one who might attempt to escape during my absence.

We set out, following up-stream the course of the Mangshan River boxed in between high cliffs which finally met at the glacier at the foot of the Mangshan Mountain, about three miles east-south-east of our camp. It was very hard to walk over the large, slippery stones, where one's feet constantly slipped and were jammed between rocks, straining and hurting the ankles. Since I did not trust my demoralized followers, who seemed on the verge of mutiny, I did not care to leave behind in camp the heavy load of silver rupees (R. 800) sewn in my coat. I always carried that sum on my person, as well as my rifle, two compasses (a prismatic and a luminous), two aneroids, one half-chronometer and another watch, and some thirty rifle cartridges. The combined weight of these articles was considerable, and on this particular afternoon it was almost too much for my strength. We travelled up and down the series of hillocks, and in and out of the innumerable channels that centuries of melting snow and ice had cut deep into the mass of loose stones. At the point where the two ranges met there stood before us the magnificent pale-green ice-terraces of the Mangshan glacier, surmounted by great snow-fields rising to the summit of the mountain range. Clouds enveloped the higher peaks. The clear ice showed vertical streaks, especially in the lower strata, where it was granulated. The base, the sides, and top of the exposed section were covered with a thick coat of snow. The Mangshan River rose from this glacier.

We left the glacier (17,800 feet above sea-level), to the right, and, turning sharply northward, began our ascent toward the pass. The snow we struggled over was so soft and deep that we sank into it up to our waists. Occasionally there was a change from snow to patches of loose débris and rotten rock. The fatigue of walking on such a surface was simply overpowering. Having climbed up half a dozen steps among the loose, cutting stones, we would slide back almost to our original point of departure, followed by a small avalanche of shifting material that only stopped when it got to the foot of the mountain.

At a height of 19,000 feet we walked for some time on soft snow, which covered an ice-field with deep crevasses and cracks. We had to feel our way with great caution, particularly as by the time we reached that spot we had only the light of the moon to depend upon.

As we rose higher, I began to feel a curious exhaustion that I had never experienced before. At sunset the thermometer which Kachi carried had fallen 40° within a few minutes, and the sudden change in the temperature seemed to affect us all. We went on, with the exception of Bijesing, who was seized with such violent mountain sickness that he was unable to proceed. The doctor, too, a powerfully built man, was suffering considerably. His legs, he said, had become like lead, and each seemed to weigh a ton. The effort of lifting, or even moving, them required all his energy. Although he was gasping pitifully for breath, he struggled on bravely until we reached an elevation of 20,500 feet. Here he was overcome with exhaustion and pain, and he was unable to go further. Kachi Ram, the Rongba, and I went ahead, but we also were suffering, Kachi complaining of violent beating in his temples and loud buzzing in his ears. He gasped and staggered dangerously, threatening to collapse at any moment. At 21,000 feet he fell flat on the snow. He was instantly asleep, breathing heavily and snoring convulsively. His hands and feet were icy cold. What caused me more anxiety than anything was the irregular beating and throbbing of his heart. I wrapped him up in his blanket and my waterproof, and, having seen to his general comfort, I shouted to the doctor (the voice in the still air carrying for a long distance) telling him what had happened. I pushed on with the Rongba, who was now the only one of the party who had any strength left.

A thick mist suddenly enveloped us, which added much to our trials. After we left Kachi at 21,000 feet we made desperate efforts to get on. Our lungs seemed about to burst, and our hearts throbbed as if they would beat themselves out of our bodies. Exhausted and weighed down by irresistible drowsiness, the Rongba and I at last reached the summit. Almost fainting with fatigue, I registered my observations. The altitude was 22,000 feet, the hour 11 P.M. There was a strong, cutting north-easterly wind. The cold was intense. I was unable to register the exact temperature, as I had forgotten to take my thermometer out of Kachi's pocket when he collapsed. The stars were wonderfully brilliant, and when the mist cleared the moon shone brightly for a while over the panorama around me. Though it was a view of utter desolation, it was certainly strangely attractive. The amount of snow on the northern slope of the range was greater than on the southern. I realized the impossibility of taking my entire expedition over this high point. Below me, to the south, were mountainous ranges buried in snow, and to the south-west and north-east were peaks even higher than the one where I stood. To the north stretched the immense, dreary Tibetan plateau with undulations and intricate hill ranges, beyond which a high mountain range with snow-peaks could just be perceived in the distance.

I had barely taken in this beautiful view of nature asleep when the mist again rose before me, and I saw a huge ghost rising out of it. A tall, dark figure stood in the centre of a luminous circle wrapped in an enormous veil of mist. The effect was wonderful. It was only after some moments that I realized that the ghost had my features, and that I stood in the centre of a circular lunar rainbow, looking at an enlarged reflection of myself in the mist. When I moved my arms, my body, or my head the ghost-like figure moved also. I felt very much like a child placed for the first time in front of a mirror, as I made the great image move about and repeat any odd motion that I might make. On a later occasion I saw a spectre, when the sun was up, with a circular rainbow round it. The moonlight effect differed from this, in that the colors of the rainbow were but faintly distinguishable.

The Rongba had fallen exhausted. I felt so faint with the unusual pressure on my lungs that, despite all the efforts to resist it, I also collapsed on the snow. The coolie and I, shivering pitifully, shared the same blanket in order to keep warm. Both of us were seized with irresistible sleepiness. I fought hard against it, for I well knew that if my eyelids once closed they would almost certainly remain so forever. The Rongba was fast asleep. I summoned my last atom of vitality to keep my eyes open. The bitter wind hissed by us. How that hiss still echoes in my ears! The Rongba crouched down, moaning through chattering teeth. His sudden shudders showed that he was in great pain. It seemed only common charity to let him have the entire blanket, which was in any case too small for both. I wrapped it tightly round his head and his doubled-up body. The exertion was too much for me. In absolute exhaustion I fell back on the snow. I made a last desperate effort to look at the glittering stars . . . my sight became dim . . .

How long this semi-consciousness lasted I do not know. "This is terrible! Doctor! Kachi!" I tried to speak. My voice seemed choked in my throat. Was what I saw before me real? On the vast white sheet of snow Kachi and the doctor lay motionless, like statues of ice, as if frozen to death. In my nightmare I tried to raise them. They were rigid. I knelt beside them, calling them, and striving with all my might to bring them back to life. Half dazed, I turned to look for Bijesing, and, as I did so, all sense of vitality seemed to freeze within me. I saw myself enclosed in a quickly contracting tomb of transparent ice. I felt that I, too, would shortly be frozen to death like my companions. My legs, my arms, were already icy. Horror-stricken as I was at the approach of such a ghastly death, I felt a languor and sleepiness far from unpleasant. Should I let myself go, choosing rest and peace rather than effort, or should I make a last struggle to save myself? The ice seemed to close in more and more every moment. I was suffocating.

I tried to scream, to force myself through the ice, which seemed to crush me. I gave a violent plunge. Then everything vanished . . . the frozen Kachi, the doctor, the transparent tomb . . .

I opened my eyes. They ached as if needles had been stuck into them. It was snowing hard. I had temporarily lost the use of my legs and fingers. They were almost frozen. In waking up from the ghastly nightmare, I realized instantly that I must get down at once to a lower level. I was already covered with a layer of snow. It was snowing hard when I woke, and I suppose it was the cold snow on my forehead that caused my nightmare. It is quite probable that, had it not been for the sudden shudder which shook me free, I should never have awakened.

I sat up with difficulty, and slowly regained the use of my lower limbs by rubbing and beating them. I roused the Rongba, rubbed him, and shook him till he was able to move. We began our descent.

Undoubtedly the satisfaction of going up high mountains is great, but can it ever be compared to the delight of coming down again?

The incline being extremely steep, we took long strides on the snow. When we came to patches of débris we slid down at a great pace amid a deafening roar from the huge mass of loose stones set in motion by our descent. It was still snowing.

"Hark!" I said to the Rongba. "What is that?"

With hands up to our ears we listened attentively.

"*Ao, ao, ao! Jaldi ao! Tumka hatte?*" (Come, come, come! Come quickly! Where are you?) cried a faint, distressed voice from far down below.

We quickened our pace. With hardly any control over our legs our descent was precipitous. The snow-fall ceased, and we became enveloped in a freezing thick mist which pierced into our very bones.

Guided by the anxious cries of the doctor, we continued

our breakneck journey downward. The cries became more and more distinct, and at last we came face to face with Wilson, still helpless.

He had been uneasy about us, and during our long absence had quite given us up for lost.

We looked for and found Kachi. He had slept like a top, curled up in his warm blanket and my waterproof coat. He was now quite refreshed. All together we continued our race downward with no serious mishaps. Life and strength gradually came back to us when we descended to lower heights.

Over the same trying stony valley we reached camp in the morning. The anxiety of my men in camp was intense. They had lost all hope of seeing us again.

CHAPTER IV

WATCHED BY SPIES

A FEW hours' rest, a hearty meal, and by 9 A.M. we were ready again to start, this time with the entire expedition, over the easier Lumpiya Pass. The thermometer registered 40° inside the tent. The minimum temperature outside, during the night, had been 14°. We followed the Kuti River at the foot of the mountain range. On rounding a prominent headland, where the Kuti River flowed through a narrow passage, we saw on a mound fourteen stone pillars and pyramids with white stones on them and some Tibetan "flying prayers," mere strips of cloth flapping in the wind. It was from this point that the ascent of the Lumpiya Pass began.

Our route gradually ascended, going north-west first, then swinging away to the north-east, until we attained an elevation of 17,350 feet on a flat basin covered with deep snow. So far we had gone on with no great trouble, but matters suddenly changed for the worse. Each coolie in the long silent row at the head of which I marched sank in snow up to his knees, often up to his waist. Their dark faces, wrapped tightly round in turbans, stood out in sharp contrast upon the white background. Some wore fur caps with ear-flaps. All had sheepskin coats and high boots. Many used snow-spectacles. Watching this silent procession of men with heavy loads upon their backs, struggling higher and higher with piteous panting, one could not help wondering anxiously as to how many of them would return to their own country alive. Moving cautiously to avoid treacherous crevasses, I made my way ahead to a spot six hundred feet higher, where I halted for a while on a rocky island fairly clear of snow. As coolie after coolie arrived panting hard, he dropped his load and sat quietly by the side of it. There was not a grumble, not a word of reproach for the hard work they were made to endure. Sleet was falling, and everything was wet and cold. From this point there was a steep pull before us. To the left we had a glacier, the face of which was a precipitous wall of ice about one hundred feet in height. Like the Mangshan glacier, it was in horizontal strata of beautifully clear ice with vertical stripes of dark green.

The doctor and I went ahead. In our anxiety to reach the summit we mistook our bearings. With great fatigue we climbed an extremely steep incline. Here we were on a patch of troublesome loose stones, on which we struggled for over half an hour, until we reached the summit of the range, 18,750 feet—considerably higher than the pass itself. Most of the other men had proceeded by a dangerous way skirting the glacier.

The wind from the north-east was piercing, and the cold intense. From this high point we obtained a beautiful bird's-eye view of the Tibetan plateau. Huge masses of snow covered the Tibetan side of the Himahlyas, as well as the lower range of mountains immediately in front of us, lying almost parallel to our range. Two thousand feet below, between these two ranges, flowed, in a wide barren valley, a river called the Darma Yankti. This river is the principal source of that great river which afterward takes the name of Sutlej. I was glad to be the first white man to visit the place where it has its birth. In the distance a flat plateau, rising some eight hundred feet above the river and resembling a gigantic railway embankment, could be seen for many miles. Far away to the north stood a chain of high blue mountains capped with snow—undoubtedly the Gangri chain with the Kelas peaks.

The strain of exertion in this rarefied air brought about a painful incident. Exhausted from cold and fatigue, a man called Rubso, a Christian convert, was seized with cramp. He was lying in a semi-conscious state, his teeth chattering, his features distorted and livid; his eyes were sunken and lifeless. We carried him under the shelter of a rock and rubbed him vigorously, endeavoring to restore his circulation. He eventually recovered enough to come along.

From our high point we now had to descend to the pass six hundred feet lower. We made our way along dangerous rocks and débris. I was clinging, with half-frozen fingers, to a prominent rock when I heard screams of distress from below. On the steep incline of snow two coolies, with their respective loads, having lost their footing, were sliding at an incredible speed. They finally reached the bottom of the basin, where the change in the descent made them turn involuntary somersaults, while their loads flew off in every direction. I was relieved when I saw the men getting up again. One of them staggered, and fell back a second time as if dead. Hastening over the slippery rocks, and then down over loose stones, I reached the pass. This was 18,150 feet above the sea. Two reluctant men were sent to the relief of the coolie in distress. He and his load were at last carried up to the place where I was. He had been badly shaken and was aching all over, but was able to continue with us.

We hurried down the steep slope on the Tibetan side, to get away quickly from the bitterly cold, windy pass. Describing a wide curve, and then across several long snow-beds, we at last reached the river-level, and pitched our tents on snow at an elevation of 16,900 feet. There was no wood; no yak or pony dung, no lichens, no moss, and therefore nothing with which we could make a fire. My men believed that eating cold food at high elevations, when the temperature was low, led to certain death. They preferred to remain without food altogether. Night came, and with it the wind blowing in gusts, and piling the grit and snow around our tents. In the night, when a hurricane was raging, we had to turn out of our flapping canvasses several times to make the loosened pegs firmer. Refastening the frozen ropes was icy-cold work. At 2 A.M. the thermometer was down to 12°; at 9 A.M., in the sun, it went up to 26°, and inside the tent at the same hour we had a temperature of 32°—freezing-point.

In a hurricane of grit and drenching rain we packed our traps as best we could and again started. To my surprise, as I was marching ahead of my men, I noticed, some two hundred yards from my former camp, a double line of recent footmarks in the snow. Those coming toward us were somewhat indistinct and nearly covered with grit; those going in the opposite direction seemed quite recent. After carefully examining these footprints, I became certain that they had been left by a Tibetan. Where the footprints were nearest our camp, marks in the snow showed that the man had at different points laid himself flat on the snow. We had evidently been spied upon and watched during the night. My men, who were already showing fear of the Tibetans, were now all anxiously stooping over these footprints. Some of them thought that the stranger must be a *daku* (a brigand), and that at night we should be attacked by the whole band; others maintained that the spy could only be a soldier sent by the Gyanema officers to watch our movements. This incident was held by them as an evil omen.

We were travelling on flat or slightly rolling barren ground. We waded across another cold river with water up to our waists. My men became so tired that one mile further we were obliged to halt. The elevation of this point was 16,650 feet.

The cold was intense. Again we had no fuel of any kind. A furious wind was blowing. Snow fell heavily in the evening. My carriers, half starved, ate a little *satoo* (a kind of oatmeal), but Chanden Sing, a Rajiput, could not, without breaking his caste, eat his food without undressing. It was two days since he had eaten his last meal, but rather than break the rules of his religion, or take off his clothes when it was so cold, he chose to curl up in his blanket and go to sleep fasting.

Inside the tent the temperature was 28° Fahrenheit, or below freezing-point. There was a foot of snow upon the ground, and it was snowing heavily. The carriers, huddled close together so as to keep warm, attempted to sleep in order to forget their hunger.

Two or three hours later the weather cleared. The coolies, half starved, came to complain that they were again unable to find fuel to cook their food, and that they would leave me. It was a trying time. I immediately took my telescope and climbed to the top of a small mound. It was curious to see how much faith the coolies had in this spy-glass. They believed, in a child-like fashion, that with it I could see through mountains. I came down with the good news that one day's march beyond would bring us to a spot where fuel was plentiful.

They cheerfully hastened to pack up the loads, and set forth with unusual energy in the direction I had pointed out. We followed a course parallel to the high, flat plateau on the other side of the stream. This snow-covered plateau extended from south-west to north-east. Beyond it to the north could be seen some high, snowy peaks—in all probability the lofty summits south-east of Gartok. To our right we were flanked by high, rugged mountains, with streams here and there dashing down their sides. Six hours' brisk marching took us to a sheltered spot where a few lichens and shrubs were growing. If we had suddenly descended into the Black Forest of Germany or the Yosemite Valley with their gigantic trees centuries old, our delight could not have been greater, yet the tallest of these shrubs stood no higher than six or seven inches from the ground, while the biggest piece of wood we collected was no larger around than an ordinary pencil. With all possible haste all hands went to work to root up these plants for fuel.

When night came the same number of hands were busy cooking and swiftly ladling out such steaming food as was available from the different pots to the mouths of the famished coolies. Happiness reigned in camp. All recent hardships were forgotten.

A fresh surprise was awaiting us when we rose. Two Tibetans disguised as beggars came to our camp. They pretended to be suffering from cold and starvation. I gave orders that they should be properly fed and kindly treated. On being cross-examined they confessed that they were spies sent by the officer at Gyanema to find out whether a white man had crossed the frontier, and whether we had seen him.

We had so many things to attend to in the morning, and it was so cold, that washing had really become a nuisance. I, for my part, gave it up, at least for the time. We were sunburnt, and we wore turbans and snow-glasses, so the Tibetans departed under the impression that our party consisted of a Hindoo doctor, his brother, and a caravan of servants (none of whom had seen a white man), and that we were now on a pilgrimage to the sacred Mansarowar Lake and Kelas Mount.

In the presence of the men we treated this as a great

joke, but, all the same, Wilson and I anxiously consulted as to our immediate plans. Should we make a rapid march during the night over the mountain range to our right, and strike east by the wilds, or should we face the Gyanema leader and his soldiers?

We decided to meet them rather than go out of our way. I gave orders to break camp at once.

CHAPTER V

WARNED BACK BY SOLDIERS

WE altered our course from north to north-east, rising to 16,600 feet. We arrived at Lama Chokten, a pass protected by a Tibetan guard. The soldiers quickly turned out, matchlocks in hand. They seemed a miserable lot. They offered no resistance, but begged for money and food. The men complained of ill-treatment from their superiors. They received no pay, and even food was only occasionally sent to them at this outpost. Their tunics were in rags. Each man carried a sword stuck in front through the girdle. Here, too, we had more inquiries about the young sahib, the white man. Messengers on horseback had been sent post-haste from Taklakot to warn the Gyanema officer not to let him penetrate into Hundes (the Tibetan name for Tibet) should he attempt to come by the Lumpiya Pass. Their description of my supposed appearance was amusing enough to me, and when they said that if the sahib came their way they would cut off his head, I felt so touched by their good-natured confidence that I wanted to distribute a few rupees among them.

"Don't give them anything, sir," said Kachi and the doctor. "These fellows are friends of the dacoits. If these get to know that you have money, we shall run great risk of being attacked by them."

I insisted on giving them a present.

"No, sir," cried Kachi; "do not do it, or it will bring us trouble and misfortune. If you give them four annas, that will be ample."

Accordingly the commanding officer had this large sum deposited in his outstretched palm. To show his satisfaction, he put out his tongue to its full length, waved both hands in sign of gratitude, bowing clumsily at the same time. His fur cap had been previously removed and thrown on the ground. It was a great deal of ceremony over a gift which amounted to somewhat less than eight cents.

From this place I saw a beautiful sight. To the north the clouds had scattered, and the snow-covered sacred Kelas Mountain rose up before us. Not unlike the graceful roof of a temple, Kelas towered over the long, white-capped range, contrasting in its beautiful blending of tints with the warm sienna color of the lower elevations. Kelas was some two thousand feet higher than the other peaks of the Gangri chain. It showed strongly defined ledges and terraces marking its stratification, and these were covered with horizontal layers of snow of brilliant white in contrast to the dark, ice-worn rock. The Tibetans, the Nepalese, the Shokas, the Humlis, Jumlis, and Hindoos, all had a strong veneration for this mountain, which was believed by them to be the abode of all the good gods, especially the god Siva. In fact, the ledge round its base was said by the Hindoos to be the mark of the ropes used by the devil "Rakas" in his effort to pull down the throne of Siva.

My men, with heads uncovered, their faces turned toward the sacred peak, were muttering prayers. With joined hands, which they slowly raised as high as the forehead, they prayed fervently, and then went down on their knees, with heads touching the ground. My brigand follower, who was standing close by me, hurriedly whispered that I should join in the prayers.

"You must keep friends with the gods," said the bandit; "misfortune will attend you if you do not bow to Kelas. That is the home of a good god!" And he pointed to the peak with the most devout air of conviction.

To please him, I saluted the mountain with great deference, and, imitating the example of my men, placed a white stone on one of the *Choktens* or *Obos* (stone pillars). Hundreds of these had been erected at this place by devotees. These Obos, or rough pyramids of stones, were to be found on the paths over high passes, near lakes, and at the source of rivers. At no place had I seen so many as at Lama Chokten. Each passer-by deposited a white stone on one of these Obos. This was supposed to bring good fortune.

The guard-house itself, of rough stone, would in any country but Tibet be recognized as better fitted for pigs than for human beings.

Having gone a mile or so further, as the sun was fast disappearing we searched for a suitable spot to pitch our tents. There was no sign of water, only the stony bed of a dried rivulet. We were discussing the situation when we heard a faint sound of rushing water. It grew louder and louder, and then we saw coming our way a stream of limpid snow-water gradually creeping over a bed of stones. Evidently the snow of the mountains, which had melted during the day, had only now reached the spot where we stood. My brigand was greatly excited.

"Water flowing to you, sahib!" he exclaimed, with his arms outstretched. "You will have great luck! Look! Look! You want water for your camp, and a stream comes to you! Heaven blesses you. You must dip your fingers into the water as soon as it comes up to you, and throw some drops over your shoulders. Fortune will then attend you on your journey."

I readily fell in with this Tibetan superstition. We all dipped our fingers and sprinkled the water over our backs. Wilson, however, who took the matter quite seriously, said it was all nonsense, and would not give in to such "childish superstitions."

In front of our camp was a great stretch of flat alluvial land, about ten miles long and fourteen wide, which apparently had once been the bed of a lake. With my telescope I could see at the foot of a small hill the camping-ground of Karko. There were many tents. My men seemed reassured when by their shape and color we made out the tents to be those of Joharis from Milam, who came over to this place to trade with the Tibetans. Beyond Karko to the north a stretch of water, the Gyanema Lake, shone brilliantly, and beyond it could be seen comparatively low hill ranges. In the distance more snowy peaks were visible.

On leaving camp we traversed the plain for six miles in a north-easterly direction, and then turned into a smaller valley well enclosed by hills, which we followed for a distance of three or four miles.

During our march we saw many herds of *kiang* (wild horse). They came close to us. They resembled zebras, except that they were light brown in color. Their graceful and coquettish ways were most attractive. The natives regarded the proximity of these animals as dangerous, for their apparent tameness was merely in order to get quite near the unwary traveller, and then, with a sudden dash, inflict a horrible bite.

Having climbed over a hill range, we descended on the other side into a grassy stretch of flat land with a lake on the northern side. On a hill south of the lake stood the Gyanema fort, a primitive, tower-like structure of stone, with a tent pitched over it to answer the purpose of a roof. Two dirty white rags hung from a flagstaff. These were not national flags, but merely wind-prayers. Lower down, at the foot of the hill, were two or three large black tents and a small shed of stone. Hundreds of black, white, and brown yaks[1] were grazing on the green patches of grass.

The appearance of our party evidently frightened everybody, for we had hardly shown ourselves on the summit of the pass when in the fort a gong began to sound loudly, filling the air with its metallic notes. A shot was fired. Soldiers with their matchlocks[2] ran here and

[1] A kind of ox with long hair.

[2] Old muskets fired by a fusee, with a prong to rest the barrel on.

there. They pulled down one of the black tents and hastily conveyed it inside the fort. The greater part of the garrison sought shelter within the walls of the fort with the hurry almost of a stampede. When, after some time, they made up their minds that we did not mean to hurt them, some of the Tibetan officers, followed by their men, came trembling to meet us. The doctor, unarmed, went ahead to talk to them, while Chanden Sing and I remained with the coolies in order to protect our baggage in case of a treacherous attack, and to prevent my frightened carriers from abandoning their loads and escaping. Matters looked peaceful enough. Rugs were spread on the grass, and finally we all sat down. An hour of tiresome talking with the Tibetan officers, while the same things were repeated over and over again, led to nothing. They said they could on no account allow any one from India, whether native or sahib, to proceed, and we must go back. We, on our side, stated that we were doing no harm. We were pilgrims to the sacred Lake of Mansarowar, only a few miles farther. We had gone to much expense and trouble. How could we now turn back when so near our goal? We would not go back, and trusted they would allow us to proceed.

We treated them courteously. Probably mistaking this for fear, they promptly took advantage of it, especially the Magbun, the General-in-Chief in charge of the Gyanema fort. His humble manner, of which at first he had made so much display, suddenly turned into arrogance.

"You will have to cut off my head," said he, with a

vicious countenance, "or, rather, I will cut off yours, before I let you go another step."

"Cut off my head!" I cried, jumping on my feet and shoving a cartridge into my rifle.

"Cut off my head!" repeated Chanden Sing, pointing with his Martini-Henry at the official.

"Cut off our heads!" exclaimed the Brahmin, angrily, and the two Christian servants of Dr. Wilson, while they handled a Winchester and a couple of Gourkha *kukris* (large knives).

"No, no, no, no! Salaam, salaam, salaam!" shouted the Magbun, with the quickness of a panic-stricken man. "Salaam, salaam," repeated he again, bowing down to the ground, tongue out, and placing his hat at our feet in a disgustingly servile manner. "Let us talk like friends."

The Magbun's men, no braver than their master, shifted about in a casual manner, so as to be behind their superior officers in case of our firing. On second thought, feeling that they were not safe even so screened, they got up. One after the other the Tibetans walked away for half-a-dozen steps slowly, to impress upon us that it was not fear that made them leave, and then took to their heels.

The Magbun and the officers who remained became meek. We spoke and argued in a friendly manner for two long hours, but with no result. The Magbun could not decide of his own accord. He would consult with his officers, and he could give us an answer no sooner than the next morning. In the mean time he would provide for our general comfort and insure our safety, if we would encamp near his tent. This, of course, I well knew to be a trick to gain time, so as to send for soldiers to Barca, north of the Rakastal Lake, as well as to all the neighboring camps. I frankly told him my suspicions, but added that I wished to deal fairly with the Tibetan authorities before resorting to force. I reminded the Magbun again and made him plainly understand that we were merely peaceful travellers, and had not come to fight; that I was paying tenfold for anything I purchased from him or his men, and was glad to do so; but at the same time, let any one beware who dared touch a single hair of a member of my party! The Magbun declared that he understood perfectly. He swore friendship, and as friends he begged us to stop over the night near his camp. By the Sun and Kunjuk Sum (Trinity) he gave a solemn oath that we should in no way be harmed. He took humble leave of us and retired.

The doctor and I had been sitting in front. Next were Chanden Sing, the Brahmin, and the two Christians. The carriers were behind. When the Magbun had gone, I turned round to look at my followers. What a sight! They one and all were crying, each man hiding his face in his hands. Kachi had tears streaming down his cheeks, Dola was sobbing, while the brigand and the other Tibetan in my employ, who had for the occasion assumed a disguise, were hiding behind their loads. Serious though the situation was, I could not help laughing at the fright of my men.

We pitched our tents. I had been sitting inside, noting

the observations which I had taken with my instruments and writing up my diary, when Kachi crept in, apparently in great distress. He seemed so upset that he could hardly speak.

"Master!" he whispered. "Master! The Tibetans have sent a man to your coolies threatening to kill them if they remain faithful to you. They must abandon you during the night. If you attempt to hold them they have orders to kill you."

At the same time that this agent had been sent to conspire with my coolies, other envoys of the Magbun brought into my camp masses of dry dung to make our fires. These men conveyed to me again the Magbun's renewed declarations of friendship. Nevertheless, soldiers were sent in every direction by the Tibetan official to call for help. I saw them start. One messenger went toward Kardam and Taklakot, a second proceeded in the direction of Barca, a third galloped to the west.

My carriers were evidently preparing to leave me. I watched them, unseen, through an opening in the tent. They were busily engaged separating their blankets and clothes from my loads, dividing the provisions among themselves, and throwing aside my goods. I went out to them, patiently made them repack the things, and warned them that I would shoot any one who attempted to revolt or desert.

While the doctor and I sat down to a hearty meal, Chanden Sing was intrusted with the preparations for war on our side. He cleaned the rifles with much care, and got the ammunition ready. He was longing to fight.

The Brahmin, on whose faithfulness we could also rely, remained cool and collected through the whole affair. He was a philosopher, and never worried over anything. He took no active part in preparing for our defence, for he did not fear death. God alone could kill him, he argued, and all the matchlocks in the country together could not send a bullet through him unless God wished it. And if it be God's decree that he should die, what would be the use of rebelling against it? The two converts, like good Christians, were more practical, and lost no time in grinding the huge blades of their *kukris*, in order to make them as sharp as razors.

When darkness came I placed a guard a little distance off our camp. It seemed likely that the Tibetans might make a rush on our tent if they had a chance. One of us kept watch all night outside the tent, while those inside lay down in their clothes, with loaded rifles by their side. I cannot say that either Dr. Wilson or I felt very uneasy, for the Tibetan soldiers, with their clumsy matchlocks, long spears, and jewelled swords and daggers, were more picturesque than dangerous.

CHAPTER VI

ENCOUNTER WITH A HIGH TIBETAN OFFICIAL

EARLY the next morning we were roused by the distant sound of tinkling horse-bells. On looking out of the tent I saw a long row of pack-ponies heavily laden, escorted by a number of mounted soldiers with matchlocks and spears. It was evident that some high official was coming. This advance-guard consisted of his inferior officers and baggage. They took a long sweep far away from our tent, and dismounted at the Gyanema fort. Other soldiers and messengers were constantly arriving in groups from all directions. The leader of one party, with a large escort of soldiers, was received with profuse salaams. I concluded that he must be an important person.

After some time a message was sent to us that this new-comer, the Barca Tarjum, wished to have the honor of seeing us. His rank might be described as that of a feudal prince. We replied that we were having our breakfast, and that we would send for him when we wished to speak to him. Our experience had taught us that it was better to treat Tibetan officials as inferiors, as they were then more subdued and easier to deal with. At eleven, we sent a messenger to the fort, to say we should be pleased to receive the Tarjum. He came immediately with a large following. He was a picturesque figure dressed in a long coat of green silk of Chinese shape, with large sleeves turned up, showing his arms up to the elbow. He had a cap similar to those worn by Chinese officials, and he was shod in heavy, long black boots, with large nails under the soles. His long, pale, angular face was remarkable in many ways. It was dignified and full of repose. Though somewhat weak, his features were rather fine. Long hair fell in loose curls down to his shoulders. Hanging from his left ear was a large ear-ring, with malachite ornaments and a pendant. In his nervous fingers he held a small roll of Tibetan material, which he used with both hands as a handkerchief. He blew his nose inconsequently every time he was at a loss to answer a question. The Tarjum and his men were profuse in their bows, and there was, as usual, a great display of tongues.

We had rugs placed outside our principal tent. The doctor and I sat on one, asking the Tarjum to sit on the one facing us. His followers squatted around him. It is a well-known fact that in Tibet, if you are a "somebody," or if you wish people to recognize your importance, you must have an umbrella spread over your head. Fortunately the ever-prudent doctor had two, and these were duly spread over our respective heads. The Tarjum himself was shaded under a parasol of colossal dimensions, held in position by his secretary.

In spite of the extravagant terms of friendship which fell from the Tarjum's lips, I was convinced, by studying the man's face, that his words were insincere, and that it would be unsafe to trust him. He never looked us straight in the face. His eyes were fixed on the ground all the time, and he spoke in an unpleasantly affected manner. I did not like the man from the very first, and, friend or no friend, I kept my loaded rifle on my lap.

After long, heavy speeches, clumsy compliments, and tender inquiries on the state of health of all relatives they could possibly think of, after repeated blowing of the nose and loud coughing, which always came on when we asked whether they had yet decided what we should be allowed to do, at last, when my patience was nearly exhausted, our negotiations of the previous day were reopened. We argued for hours. We asked to be allowed to go on. They were still uncertain whether they would let us or not. To simplify matters, and hasten their decision before other reinforcements arrived, the doctor applied for permission to let only eight of us proceed to Mansarowar.. He (the doctor) himself would remain at Gyanema with the rest of the party, as a proof of good faith. Even this offer they rejected, not directly, but with hypocritical excuses and delays. They thought we could not find our way, and that if we did we should find it rough and the climate too severe; that brigands might attack us, and so on. All this was tiresome. The Tibetans were even getting unpleasant. I decided to bring matters to a crisis.

Still holding the rifle cocked at safety on my lap, I turned the muzzle of it toward the Tarjum, and purposely let my hand slide down to the trigger. He became uncomfortable. His face showed signs of apprehension.

His eyes, until now fixed on the ground, became first unsteady, and then settled fixedly, with a look of distress, on the muzzle of my rifle. He tried to dodge the aim, right or left, by moving his head. I made the weapon follow his movements. The Tarjum's servants fully shared their master's fear. Without doubt the poor fellow was in agony; his tone of voice, a moment before loud and insulting, now became very humble. With much meekness he expressed himself ready to please us in every way.

"I see that you are good people," said he, in a faint whisper accompanied by a deep bow. "I cannot give, as I should like, my official approval to your journey forward, but you can go if you wish. I cannot say more. Eight of you can proceed to the sacred Mansarowar Lake. The others will remain here."

Before giving his final decision, he said that he would prefer to have another consultation with his officers.

We granted this readily.

The Tarjum then presented the doctor with a roll of Tibetan cloth.

I had bathed in the morning, and my Turkish towel was spread outside the tent to dry. The Tarjum, who showed great interest in all our things, took a particular fancy to its knotty fabric. He sent for his child to see this wonderful material, and when he arrived the towel was placed on the youth's back as if it were a shawl. I at once offered it to him as a present if he would accept it. There were no bounds to his delight, and our relations, somewhat strained a few minutes earlier, became now of the friendliest character. We invited the party inside our tent, and they examined everything with curiosity, asking endless questions. They were now quite pleasant, and even amusing. Tibetans have a craving for alcohol. They soon asked if I had any to give them; there was nothing they would like more. As I never carry intoxicants, I could not offer whiskey, wine, or beer; but, not wishing to disappoint them, I produced a bottle of methylated spirit[1] (which I used as fuel in my hypsometrical[2] apparatus). This they readily drank, apparently liking its throat-burning-qualities. They even asked for more. The Tarjum complained of an ailment from which he had suffered for some time. The doctor was able to give him a suitable remedy. All officers received small presents. Then they departed.

In the afternoon a messenger came from the Barca Tarjum. He had good news for us. The Tarjum wished us to understand that, "as we had been so kind to him and his followers, he regarded us as his personal friends. As we were so anxious to visit the Mansarowar Lake and the great Kelas Mount, and had already experienced many difficulties and great expense in coming so far, he agreed that eight of our party should proceed to these sacred places. It was impossible for him to give an official consent, but he repeated again that we could go if we wished."

This news naturally delighted me. Once at Kelas, I felt sure I could easily go further.

On the same evening a traitor in our camp sneaked

[1] Purified alcohol. [2] See Chapter I.

from under the tent in which my men were sleeping and paid a visit to the Tarjum. There is no doubt that he told him I was not the doctor's brother nor a Hindoo pilgrim. He disclosed that I was a sahib, and that I was on my way to Lhassa. From what I heard afterward, it seemed that the Tarjum did not quite believe his informant; but, fresh doubts arising in his mind, he sent a message in the night, entreating us to return the way we had come.

"If there is really a sahib in your party, whom you have kept concealed from me, and I let you go on, my head will be cut off by the Lhassa officials. You are now my friends, and you will not allow this."

"Tell the Tarjum," I replied to the messenger, "that he is my friend, and I will treat him as a friend."

In the morning we found thirty horsemen, fully armed, posted about one hundred yards from our tent. To go ahead with my frightened men and be followed by this company would certainly bring trouble. It was better to adopt other tactics.

Much to the astonishment of the armed force and their superiors, the doctor, Chanden Sing, and I, rifles in hand, walked firmly toward the company of soldiers. After us came the trembling coolies. The Magbun and the Tarjum's officers could hardly believe their eyes. The soldiers quickly dismounted and laid their weapons down, to show that they had no intention of fighting. We passed without taking notice of them. The Magbun ran after me. He begged me to stop one moment. A pair of prettily embroidered cloth boots were produced from the loose folds of the official's coat, and he offered them to me with the following words:

"Though your face is sunburnt and black, and your eyes are sore" (they were not, as a matter of fact, but I wore snow-spectacles), "your features tell me that you are of good family. You must be a high officer in your country. Your noble feelings also show that you would not have us punished for your sake, and now our hearts are glad to see you retrace your steps. Let me offer you these boots, so that your feet may not get sore on the long and difficult journey back to your native land."

It was neatly put, though the mode of reasoning was peculiar. I accepted the boots. The Magbun and his guard salaamed to the ground.

Without further parleying we left the Magbun, and, retracing our steps, proceeded in a west-south-west direction, as though we had decided to turn back and leave the country.

We reached the summit of the hill and crossed to the other side. My men went on down the slope, but I remained, hidden behind a large stone, to observe with my telescope the people at Gyanema. No sooner had my last man disappeared on the other side of the pass than the cavalrymen jumped into their saddles, and, raising clouds of dust, galloped after us. This was what I had expected. I hastened to rejoin my men. When down in the plain, I again took my telescope and watched the sky-line of the hill we had just descended. Some thirty heads could be seen peeping over the rocks from among the boulders. The soldiers had evidently dismounted and were spying our movements. I felt annoyed that they did not openly follow us. I sighted my rifle to eight hundred yards, lay down flat, and took aim at a figure I could see more plainly than the others.

The doctor snatched the rifle from my shoulder.

"You must not shoot," said he, with his usual calmness; "you might kill somebody."

"I only wish to teach those cowards a lesson."

"That is all very well. But every man in Tibet is so cowardly that the lesson would have to be constantly repeated," answered Wilson, with his unfailing wisdom.

I slung my rifle over my shoulder, and made up my mind to start some other time on the great task I had then so nearly begun.

When we had covered a mile or so of the plain our ghostly escort crossed the pass, and came full gallop down the hill. I gave orders to my men to halt. The soldiers also came to a dead stop. I watched them through the telescope. They seemed to be holding a discussion. At last five men rode full speed northward, probably to guard the track in that direction. Three men remained where they were, and the remainder, as if seized by panic, galloped frantically up the hill again and disappeared over the summit.

We resumed our march. The three horsemen followed a course one mile south of ours, close against the foot of the hills. Lying low upon their ponies' heads, they probably imagined that they were passing us unperceived. Seeing that our bearings were for our old camp at Lama Chokten, they left our line and rode ahead of us.

When, in the evening, we reached Lama Chokten two shepherds came to greet us. Then another appeared.

"Our sheep are far away," said they. "We are hungry. We are poor. Can we stop near your camp and pick up the food that you will throw away?"

"Certainly," I replied. "But mind you do not pick up anything else."

These simple people, thinking I should not know them, had left their ponies at the Lama Chokten guard-house, and, disguised as shepherds, were now trying to make friends with us, with the object of discovering our movements. They were, of course, the three sepoys from Gyanema in disguise.

At each step in our retreat toward the Himahlyas my heart became heavier. I was thinking out fresh plans, but to think out plans and to carry them into effect were two different matters.

How many times had my schemes been upset! How often had I been forced to begin afresh when all seemed to point toward success! Now things had changed altogether for the worse. My chances of success, notwithstanding my constant struggle, were getting smaller and smaller every day. Failure stared me in the face.

At this camp the *daku* (brigand), who had changed his disguise several times since coming in contact with the Tibetans, announced his immediate departure. The doctor, with his usual kindness, had already begged him to remain, but without avail. We well knew that in this region, infested by robbers, this man was only leaving us to become a robber again. The *daku* knew that I carried a large sum of money. During the last two days his behavior had been more than strange. Had he come across some of his mates, or had he heard from the soldiers that they were in the neighborhood?

The *daku* had a bundle of blankets strapped on his back in readiness to leave me. My men, distressed at this new danger, came to report it to me. I sent for him. Speaking bluntly, and keeping his eyes fixed on the ground, he said:

"I am going, sahib."

"Where?" I inquired.

"I have friends near here, and I am going to them."

"Very good, go," I replied, calmly taking up my rifle.

His load was off his shoulders in less time than it takes to tell of it. He resumed his work as usual. One or two other riotous coolies were brought back to reason in a similar manner.

I heard later that a band of brigands attacked a party of traders near the frontier two days after this occurred.

Another painful march back! We went a few miles and encamped on the bank of a rapid stream, the Shirlangdu. From this point, with some difficulty, it would be possible to climb over the mountain range during the night, and attempt to elude the spies and watchmen by crossing the mountains as far as Lake Mansarowar. I made up my mind to attempt this. It seemed to add to the risk to have so large a following as thirty men, so I decided that only four or five should accompany me. Going alone was impossible, because of the difficulty of carrying sufficient food. Nevertheless, if the worst came to the worst, I resolved to attempt going absolutely alone and rely on the chance of obtaining food from Tibetans.

All the loads were rearranged. Articles of clothing and comfort, niceties in the way of food, and extras in the way of luxuries were left behind to make room for my scientific instruments.

Each pound in weight dedicated to science meant a pound less food to take us to Lhassa. Everything that was not strictly necessary had to be left behind.

Two Tibetan spies came to camp in the afternoon in the disguise, as usual, of beggars. They asked for food and insisted upon it. Their manner was unbearably insulting. This was a little too much for us. Bijesing, the Johari, and Rubso, the Christian cook, were the first to enter into an open fight with them. They punched and kicked them, driving them down a steep ravine leading to a river; then, assisted by other men in camp, showered stones upon them.

CHAPTER VII

AN EXCITING NIGHT JOURNEY

THE hour fixed for my flight was 9 P.M. Five men had been induced to follow me by the offer of a handsome reward.

At the appointed hour no one had put in an appearance. I went in search of them. One man had purposely injured his feet and was disabled, another professed to be dying, the others positively refused to accompany me. All were shivering with fright and cold.

"Kill us, sahib, if you like," they implored of me, "but we will not follow you."

At 3 A.M. all attempts to get even one man to carry a load had proved futile. I had to abandon the idea of starting.

My prospects became gloomier than ever. Another march back toward the cold and dreary pass by which I had entered Tibet!

"You are depressed, Mr. Landor," remarked the doctor.

I admitted the fact. Every step backward was to me like a stab in the heart. My only wish was to push on at any cost, and it was only on account of my good friend, the doctor, that I had reluctantly refrained from making my way onward by force. My blood was boiling. The cowardice of my men made them so contemptible in my eyes that I could not bear even to look at them.

On this depressing march I walked alone ahead of my party. The rugged way seemed short and easy. I found a suitable spot for our camp. Before me and on every side stood high, snowy mountains. In front towered that same Lumpiya Pass over which I had crossed into Tibet when my spirits ran high and I had hopes of taking my entire expedition toward the sacred city of Lhassa. I now hated the sight of those mountains.

Whether it is that storms come when one is depressed, or whether one gets depressed when storms approach, I am not prepared to say. On this occasion, when I was indeed very depressed, and before we had time to pitch our tents, the wind, which had been high all through the afternoon, increased tenfold. The clouds became black and threatening, and snow soon fell in feathery flakes.

"What are you going to do?" inquired the doctor of me. "I think you had better return to Garbyang, get fresh men, and make another start."

"No, doctor. I will die rather than continue this backward march. I have resolved to start alone to-night. I am convinced that I shall have better success. I shall find my way over the range."

"No, no, it is impossible, Mr. Landor!" cried the doctor, with tears in his eyes. "That must mean death to any one attempting it."

I told him I was quite determined to go.

The poor doctor was dumfounded. He knew that it was quite useless to try to dissuade me. I went into the tent to rearrange my baggage, making the load I intended to carry on my back as light as possible. My scientific instruments, money, and cartridges already made a good weight to carry on my person.

While I was making preparations for my journey Kachi Ram entered the tent. He looked perplexed.

"What are you doing, sir?" he inquired. "The doctor says you are going to leave alone to-night, cross the mountain range, and go to Lhassa by yourself."

"Yes; that is true."

"Oh, sir, the perils and dangers are too great! You cannot go."

"I know; but I am going to try."

"Oh, sir, then I will come with you."

"No, Kachi. You will suffer too much. Go back to your father and mother, now that you have the opportunity."

"No, sir; where you go, I will go. Small men never suffer. If they do, it does not matter. Only great men's sufferings are worth noticing. If you suffer, I will suffer. I will come."

Kachi's philosophy touched me. He meant what he said. I decided to take him.

This was a piece of luck. Kachi Ram had five bosom friends among the young Shoka coolies. In the evenings in camp they often joined in weird love-songs, in memory of the fair maids of their hearts whom they had left behind, on the other side of the Himahlyas.

Kachi hurried away in a state of great excitement. He was back in a few minutes.

"How many coolies will you take, sir?"

"None will come."

"Oh, I will get them," said he, with assurance. "Will five do?"

"Yes," I murmured, incredulously.

My doubt sustained a shock when Kachi returned, buoyant, saying, in his peculiar English:

"Five Shokas come, sir. Then you, sir, I, sir, five coolies, sir, start night-time. What clock?"

"By Jove, Kachi," I could not help exclaiming, "you are a smart lad!"

"'Smart,' sir?" inquired he, sharply, hearing a new word. He was most anxious to learn English, and he had a mania for spelling. "'Smart!' What is meaning? How spell?"

"S-m-a-r-t. It means 'quick, intelligent.'"

"Smart," he repeated, solemnly, as he wrote the newly acquired word into a book which I had given him for the purpose. Kachi was undoubtedly, in spite of small faults, a great character. He was a most intelligent, sharp, well-meaning fellow. His never-failing good-humor and his earnest desire to learn and to be useful were quite refreshing.

My luck seemed to have turned. A few minutes later Chanden Sing, quite unaware that any one had undertaken to accompany me, entered the tent, and exclaimed, in a disgusted manner:

"*Shoka crab, sahib! Hunya log bura crab. Hazur, hum, do admi jaldi Lhassa giao*" (The Shokas are bad. The Hunyas are very bad. Your honor and I, we two alone, will go quickly by ourselves to Lhassa).

Here was another plucky and useful man anxious to come. He professed to have no fear of death. How true the poor fellow's words were we will learn later.

Chanden Sing was a man of strong sporting tastes. His happiness was complete when he could fire his rifle at something, though he was never known to hit the mark. He had been severely scolded and punished only a few days before for wasting several cartridges trying to shoot *kiang* (wild horse) three miles distant. Ordinary work, however, such as doing his own cooking or keeping my things tidy, was distasteful to him, and was invariably passed on to others.

Mansing, the leper, being unfortunately of the same caste as Chanden Sing, became my servant's servant. The two Hindoos constantly quarrelled and fought, but at heart they were the best of friends. The bearer, by means of promises, mingled at intervals with blows, eventually succeeded in inducing his protégé to join in our new expedition and face what dangers we might find ahead.

By eight o'clock in the evening I had collected all the men who had promised to follow me. They comprised my bearer, Kachi, and six coolies.

We named this camp "Devil's Camp," for diabolical indeed was the wind that shook our tents, not to speak of the snow blown into our shelters by the raging storm. During the night the wind grew in fury. Neither wood, dung, nor lichens for fuel could be found. Our tents were pitched at 16,900 feet above sea-level. To ascend to the summit of the range would mean a further climb of two thousand feet. In such weather the difficulties of the ascent were increased tenfold, though for escaping the notice of the Tibetan watchmen, who were spying our movements, we could have no better chance than on a stormy night like this. I arranged with the doctor that he was to take back to Garbyang all the baggage I had discarded and the men who had declined to follow me. He must leave all our tents pitched until the afternoon of the next day, in order to let the Tibetans suppose that we were all sheltered under them. This would give me time to make a long forced march before they could discover that I had left my tent, and could get on my track. Hard as it would be for our little party going forward, we would take no tent except the small *tente d'abri*, which weighed about four pounds. We should, in any case, be unable to pitch a tent for several days, for fear of being detected by the Tibetans. As soon as they would discover that we had left they would surely start in search of us. We should have to march long distances at night, keeping mostly on the summit of the range instead of proceeding, like ordinary travellers, along the valleys. We must get what little sleep we could during the day, when we could hide in some secluded spot. The thought of making a fire had to be abandoned because, even in the remote chance of finding fuel at the great altitudes where we were compelled to camp, every one knows that the light of a fire and a column of smoke can be seen from great distances, both in the day and at night. We had talked over all these matters before we made a start, and, moreover, we were fully aware that if the Tibetans could lay their hands upon us, we were too few to fight them, and we had little chance of escaping with our lives. In fact, taking things all round, we had come to the conclusion that our lives were worth a mere song from the moment of our leaving Devil's Camp.

With the full knowledge of what we were undertaking we may have been foolish in starting at all, but lack of determination cannot fairly be charged against us.

The thoughtful doctor had brought with him from our last camp a few lichens, with which he was now attempting to light a fire to cook me a few *chapatis* (native flat breads of India). Alas! four hours' hard work and four entire boxes of matches failed to produce the semblance of a flame.

At midnight I sent Chanden Sing and Kachi to collect the men. Two came trembling into the tent, the others could not be roused. I went myself and took them, one by one, to their loads. All were crying like children. It was then that I discovered that in the haste and confusion I had made one load too many. Here was a dilemma! Everything was ready and propitious for our flight. A delay at this juncture was fatal. I must have another man.

The moans and groans in the coolies' tent, when I went in search of another volunteer, were pitiful. You might have thought that they were all going to die, and this was their last agony. All because of the terror of being picked out to follow me.

At last, after threats and promises, Bijesing, the Johari, was persuaded to come. But the load was too heavy for

AT NIGHT I LED MY MEN UP THE MOUNTAIN IN A FIERCE SNOW-STORM

him; he would only carry half. To save trouble, I agreed to carry the other half myself in addition to my own load.

We put out our hurricane-lantern, and at 2 P.M., when the gale was raging at its height, driving the grit and snow like spikes into our faces, when the wind and cold seemed to penetrate with biting force to the marrow of our bones, a handful of silent men, half frozen and staggering, left the camp to face the blizzard. I ordered my men to keep close together, and we made immediately for the mountain-side, taking care to avoid the places where we supposed the Tibetan spies were posted.

We could not have selected a more suitable night for our escape. It was so dark that we could not see more than a few inches in front of us. The doctor, in sad silence, accompanied me for a couple of hundred yards. I urged him to return to the tent. He stopped to grasp my hand. In a broken voice the good man gave me his blessing, and bade me farewell.

"The dangers of your journey," whispered Dr. Wilson, "are so great and so numerous that God alone can guide you through. When I think of the cold, hunger, and hardships you will have to endure I can but tremble for you."

"Good-bye, doctor," said I.

"Good-bye," he repeated. "Good . . . ." and his voice failed him. We parted.

Two or three steps, and the darkness separated us. His touching words of farewell rang sadly in my ears as I remembered the loyalty and thoughtfulness of this good friend.

The journey toward Lhassa had recommenced in grim earnest. In a short while our ears, fingers, and toes were almost frozen, and the snow, fast-driven by the gale, beat mercilessly against our faces. Our eyes ached. We might have been blind for all we could see. Feeling our way with our feet, we proceeded speechless and exhausted, rising slowly higher and higher on the mountain-side. As we reached greater elevations it grew colder, and the wind became more piercing. Every few minutes we were compelled to halt and sit close together in order to warm ourselves and get fresh breath. The air was so rarefied that we could barely proceed under our heavy loads.

We heard a whistle and faint sounds like distant voices. My men collected round me, whispered "*Daku! daku!*" (Brigands! brigands!), and then threw themselves flat on the snow. I loaded my rifle and went ahead, trying in vain to perceive the enemy in the darkness. I screened my ear with one hand. Hark! . . . hark! . . . Yet another shrill whistle!

My Shokas were terrified. The sound seemed to come from directly in front of us. We immediately altered our course, wending our way upward slowly and steadily until we found ourselves at sunrise near the mountain-top. It was still snowing hard. One final effort brought us to the summit of the plateau.

Here we felt comparatively safe. Thoroughly exhausted, we deposited our burdens on the snow, and laid ourselves down close to one another, piling on the top of us all the available blankets in order to keep warm.

CHAPTER VIII

HUNGRY FUGITIVES

AT 1 P.M. we woke up, drenched to the skin, for the sun, which had come out after the storm had abated, had thawed the thick coating of snow over us. The elevation of this camp, according to my aneroids, was 18,000 feet. The wind, from the south-east, cut like a knife, and we suffered from it, not only on this occasion, but every day during the whole time we were in Tibet. This wind began to blow with great fierceness and regularity at one o'clock every afternoon, and it was only toward eight o'clock in the evening that it sometimes abated and gradually ceased. Frequently, however, the wind, instead of dropping at this time, increased in violence, blowing with terrible force during the whole night.

As we were making ready to start again, with limbs cramped and stiff, the sky again became suddenly covered with heavy gray clouds, and fresh snow fell. There was no possibility of making a fire, so we started hungry and half frozen, following a course of 70° (b.m.). We waded up to our waists through a freezingly cold stream, and, climbing steadily higher and higher for a distance of six miles, we at last reached another and loftier plateau to the north-east of the one where we had camped in the morning. The elevation of this second plateau was

18,960 feet. I was surprised to find four lakes of considerable size close to one another on this high table-land. The sun, breaking for a moment through the clouds, shone on the snow-covered tops of the surrounding mountains, silvering the water of the lakes, and displaying before us a wild and beautiful scene.

We were too hungry and tired to care greatly for beautiful sights. All we thought of was to find, as quick as possible, a suitable place where we could rest our wearied bodies, either under the shelter of the higher hills around the plateau or in one of the depressions in the ground. I was anxious to push across the plateau and descend on the north-east side to a lower altitude, where we might likely find fuel, but my men, half starved and fagged, would go no farther. Their loads, now soaking wet, were considerably heavier than under ordinary circumstances. We were all panting on account of the thin air at that great height. No sooner had we come to a partially sheltered spot between the larger lake and the most eastern sheet of water of the group than my men collapsed and said they were unable to proceed. I was concerned about them. They refused to take cold food, believing it would cause their death. I could not see how they could recover sufficient strength for the next day's marching unless I kept them properly fed. By promising that they should not die, I finally persuaded them to eat a little *satoo* (flour) and *ghur* (sweet paste). Unluckily, no sooner had they eaten some of the mixture, upon which they drank cold water, than nearly all were seized with violent pains in their stomachs, of which they complained most of the night.

Experience had taught these mountaineers that eating cold food at great elevations was more dangerous than eating no food at all. I regretted my ill-timed, if kindly meant, advice. One is apt to judge other people by one's self. Personally I never found any different effects from hot or cold food, plentiful or not, at high elevations, on the sea-level, or at intermediate altitudes.

Soon after sunset the cold was intense. It was still snowing hard. Our wet garments and blankets were beginning to freeze. I lighted a small spirit-lamp, round which we all sat close together, making such a shelter as we could with our frozen wraps. I even attempted to cook some concentrated broth on the flame, but, owing to the high altitude, the water took a long time to lose its chill, not to speak of the time it took to boil. When it was just getting tepid the flame went out, and I could not afford more spirits of wine to light the flame again. So the cooking had to be abandoned, and as the night grew colder and colder, we huddled together under our respective blankets in order to sleep. We had made a protecting wall with our baggage. My men covered their heads with their blankets, but I never could adopt their style of sleeping, as it seemed to smother me. I always slept with my head uncovered, for not only could I breathe more freely, but I wished to be on the alert should we at any time be surprised by the Tibetans. My men moaned and groaned and their teeth chattered during the night. I woke many times with a bad pain in my ears, caused by frost-bite; my eyes, too, suffered as the eyelashes became covered with icicles. Every time I tried to open my eyelids there was an uncomfortable feeling, as if the eyelashes were being torn off. In the intense cold the lids became fast frozen directly they were closed.

At last the sun rose. The night had seemed endless. When I tried to raise the blanket in order to sit up, it seemed of an extraordinary weight and stiffness. No wonder! It was frozen hard, was as rigid as card-board, and covered over with a layer of snow one foot thick. The thermometer during the night had gone down to 24°.

I called my men. They were hard to wake. They were entirely buried under the snow.

"*Uta! uta! uta!*" (Get up! get up! get up!) I called, shaking one by one, brushing off the snow from over their blankets.

"*Baroff bahut*" (There is much snow), remarked one man, as he put his nose outside his blanket and rubbed his eyes, smarting from the white glare of the snow around us. "Salaam, sahib," he added, when, having overcome his first surprise, he perceived me, and he raised his hand gracefully up to his forehead.

The others behaved in a similar manner. Kachi was, as usual, the last one to wake.

"Oh, Kachi," I shouted, "get up!"

"*Oh, bahiyoh!*" (Oh, father!) yawned he, stretching his arms. Half asleep, half awake, he looked round as if in a trance, muttering incoherent words.

"Good-morning, sir. Oh . . . much snow. Oh . . . look, sir, two *kiangs* there! What is '*kiang*' in English?"

"Wild horse."

"'Wild' you spell w-i-l-d?"

"Yes."

Here the note-book was produced from under his pillow, and the English word duly written down.

Odd creatures, these Shokas! The average European, half starved and frozen, would hardly give much thought to exact spelling under such trying circumstances.

Poor Mansing, the leper, suffered terribly. He groaned pitiably through the entire night. I had given him one of my wrappers, but his circulation had been badly affected by the intense cold. His face was gray and cadaverous, with deep lines engraved upon it from suffering. His feet were so frozen that it took him some time before he could stand upon them.

Again the Shokas would eat nothing because snow was still falling. We started toward the north-east. After a mile of flat we began a steep descent over unpleasant, loose débris and sharp rocks. The progress was rapid but painful. Looking at the country below through my telescope, I saw shrubs and lichens far down in the valley to the north-east, and also a tent and some sheep. This was unfortunate, for we had to alter our course in order not to be seen. We again climbed up to the top of the plateau and went around its summit unperceived, striking a more easterly route. Toward sunset we began our descent from the latter point. We crossed the river with no great difficulty. Having selected a nicely sheltered depression in the ground, I pitched my little tent there, by the side of a pond of melted snow. We all set out collecting lichens and shrubs in order to make a fire, and each man carried into camp several loads of fuel. In a moment we had three big fires blazing, and not only were we able to cook an excellent dinner and drown our past troubles in abundance of steaming tea, but we also managed to dry our clothes and blankets. The relief we obtained from the warmth of these fires was wonderful. In our comparative happiness we forgot the hardships and sufferings we had so far encountered. With the exception of a handful of *satao*, this was the first solid meal we had eaten during the last forty-eight hours. In those two days we had travelled twenty miles, each of us carrying a weight averaging over sixty pounds.

We were now at an elevation of 16,500 feet, which seemed quite low after our colder and loftier camping-grounds. The reaction was pleasant, and, as far as I was concerned, the outlook had changed from one of deepest depression to a condition of comparative cheerfulness and contentment.

In front of us, to the north-east, was a high mountain. —Farther toward the east could be seen a narrow valley between two hill ranges, while a river passed through a picturesque gorge in the direction of the Mangshan Mountain.

It was necessary for me to proceed along the valley to the east, for in so doing we should save ourselves trouble, time, and exertion, though perhaps we might meet Tibetans, especially bands of robbers. This part of the Nari Khorsum province was said to be infested with brigands. We had, therefore, to proceed cautiously, especially as my Shokas seemed quite afraid. We had hardly gone half a mile over the rolling country, and I had stopped behind my men to take observations with my prismatic compass, when my carriers suddenly threw themselves flat on the ground and began to retreat, crawling on hands and knees.

"*Daku! daku!*" (Brigands! brigands!) they whispered, as I got near them.

It was too late. We had been detected, and a number of dacoits, armed with matchlocks and swords, came rapidly toward us. It has always been my experience that, in such cases, the worst thing to do is to run away, for nothing encourages a man more to attack you than to show that you are afraid. I therefore loaded my Mannlicher rifle. My bearer did likewise with the Martini-Henry. I gave orders to the Shokas to squat down by their respective loads and to remain still. My bearer and I strolled toward the fast-approaching band, now less than a hundred yards distant. I shouted to them to stop. Chanden Sing signalled to them to go back. They took no notice of our warnings, and came on all the faster toward us. Undoubtedly they thought that we were merely Shoka traders, and expected to find an easy prey. They had conceived a good plan of attack. When they prepared to rush us, on getting near enough, they separated with the obvious intention of attacking us on all sides.

"*Dushu! Dushu!*" (Go back! Go back!) I cried angrily at them, raising my rifle to my shoulder and taking a steady aim at the leader. Chanden Sing did the same with one of the other men. This seemed to have a good effect upon them, for they immediately made a comical salaam and took to their heels, Chanden Sing and I pursuing them for some distance in order to get them well out of the way. We watched them from a mound close by, and discovered that a short distance off these robbers had many companions, as well as some three thousand sheep, presumably the results of their last robbery. We motioned to them to get away from our course, and finally, driving their sheep before them, they went off in the direction I pointed out to them. When they were clear of us, and my Shokas, who thought their last hour had come, had partly recovered from their fright, we proceeded on our journey, entering the narrow valley between the two hill ranges which I have already mentioned.

That we were now in a much-frequented region could be plainly seen by the numerous camping-grounds along the stream. Our success of the morning had raised our spirits, and we marched merrily, keeping to the left bank of the watercourse. A steep climb brought us to a plateau at an altitude of 16,400 feet, from which we obtained a fine view of the snow range, running east to west from the Mangshan Mountain to the Lippu Pass, and beyond, to the north-east, the four lofty peaks of Nimo Nangil, 25,360 feet, 22,200 feet, 22,850 feet, 22,670 feet high. This plateau sloped gently, and was broken by many deep crevasses, conveying the waterflow down into the Gakkon River.

On the lower portion of this plateau, and then along the course of the river, a track ran from Gyanema to

Taklakot *via* Kardam and Dogmar, and another seldom-frequented track to Mangshan, south-south-west of this place. The edge of the plateau was 15,800 feet above sea-level, and the river 550 feet lower.

This was for us a dangerous spot, as by this time the Tibetans must be aware that I had escaped and that I was well into their country. I knew that soldiers and spies must be guarding all the tracks and searching for us. This thoroughfare, being more frequented than the others, was all the more insecure. We had to display great caution in order to avoid detection. In Tibet the atmosphere is so clear that moving objects can plainly be seen very far away. I looked everywhere through my telescope, but could see no one, so we went on. My men thought it safer to descend into one of the numerous creeks, where we should be less exposed, but we had hardly reached the border of one of these when we heard noises rising from the valley below.

Crawling on our stomachs, my bearer and I peeped over the edge of the plateau. Some five hundred feet below was a Tibetan encampment, with a number of yaks and ponies grazing. Unnoticed, I watched them for some time. There were several soldiers, most probably posted there on the lookout for me. With my spy-glass I recognized some of the Gyanema men. We deemed it wise to select a spot where we could hide until night came. After dark we descended to the river (15,250 feet), scrambled across it, and made our way up a narrow gorge between high cliffs until we came to a well-hidden spot, where we halted. Followed by my men, I climbed up from rock to rock on the cliff to our left, and found a small natural platform, sheltered by a huge bowlder projecting over it. This seemed a safe enough spot for camping. We dared not put up a tent, and we took the precaution of burying all our baggage in case of a surprise during the night. Unhampered, we should at any moment be able to hide ourselves away from our pursuers or run before them. We could always come back afterward for our things if we had the chance.

Now that everything seemed to be running smoothly, I made a painful discovery. It was necessary for me to move rapidly. Imagine my surprise when I found that we were out of provisions. Before leaving the larger body of my expedition, I had given orders to my men to take food for ten days. The doctor, who had been deputed to see to this, had assured me that the loads contained quite enough to last us fully and above that length of time. Now, for some unknown reason, we had only sufficient food for one meagre meal. We only had a few grains of salt left.

"What have you done with it?" I inquired, angrily, as it immediately flashed across my mind that my carriers had been playing foul. I had ordered each man to take one pound of salt.

"Yes, sahib; but we forgot to take it," said the men, in a chorus.

After the hardships and fatigue we had undergone, and the anxiety and difficulty of carrying on my work of surveying, photography, sketching, and writing, under conditions of unusual discomfort and risk, it was indeed a

BEHIND OUR BULWARKS

hard blow to me to see my plans spoiled. We were still three or four days' journey from Mansarowar, where I expected to obtain fresh supplies. Again I had the choice of giving up and returning into India or of being captured by the Tibetan soldiers, whom I had so far successfully avoided. Though not usually affected by physical pain, I sometimes suffer under mental stress. I felt ill and depressed. To add bodily discomfort to my moral sufferings, I slipped, while jumping in the semi-darkness from stone to stone across the Gakkon River, and fell flat into about four feet of ice-cold water. The wind was high at the time. The thermometer, after dark, went down to 26°. While I was sitting in my wet clothes and talking our situation over, I became so cold and exhausted that I felt I was about to collapse altogether. High fever set in, and I became almost delirious. With my teeth chattering and my temperature at its highest, all my troubles seemed greater than they were. Failure seemed inevitable, my position hopeless. A plan suddenly flashed across my mind. Four of my men should go disguised, two as traders and two as beggars, into the Takla fort (locally called *Takla khar* or *Taklakot*), and buy food from my enemies. We, in camp, would remain hidden until they returned. I spoke to my followers, and, after some natural reluctance, four Shokas undertook to perform the daring duty. Discovery would mean to them the loss of their heads, in all probability preceded by cruel tortures. Although these men eventually betrayed me, I cannot help giving them credit for the pluck and fidelity they showed on that particular occasion.

During the night my men were particularly good to me. We did not sleep for fear of being surprised by the Tibetan soldiers. We passed hour after hour listening to Shoka stories of brigands and barbarous Tibetan tortures. Little I knew then what was in store for me. Early in the morning, when it grew light, we gathered a quantity of nettles, which were plentiful near this camp, and having boiled them thoroughly, we made of them a hearty if not quite an appetizing meal. They did not seem unpalatable at the time, and had we possessed salt to add taste and digestibility to our prickly diet, we might have felt quite happy. We supplied the deficiency by mixing with them a double quantity of pepper. At any rate, it was a relief to know that, while nettles lasted near our camp, we should at least not die of starvation.

CHAPTER IX

AN ATTEMPT AT MUTINY

THE entire food-supply for my men was now reduced to four pounds of flour, two pounds of rice, and two pounds of *sato*. This we gave to the four men who were to attempt to enter Taklakot. Their journey would be long and fatiguing. For us there were plenty of nettles to fall back upon. For myself I had a small quantity of tinned provisions, but I intended to keep these for worse days which, I feared, were in store for me.

I carefully instructed the four Shokas how to enter the Tibetan fort one by one in their disguises, and, in order to avoid suspicion, purchase only in small quantities at a time the provisions we required. When a sufficient amount was obtained to make one load, a man should immediately start back for our camp. The others were to follow separately for a few marches. At a given spot they would all four meet again and return together to us. It was exciting work to prepare the different disguises and arrange for everything. At last, after repeated good-byes and words of encouragement, the four messengers left on their perilous errand. All seemed quiet around us, so quiet that I unburied my sextant and artificial horizon and was taking astronomical observations when a herd of over a hundred yaks appeared on the pass north of our camp, and slowly advanced toward us. Were we discovered? Were the Tarjum's men coming, preceded by their animals? No time was to be lost. Instruments and blankets were quickly cleared away and hidden. Crawling up toward the animals, that had stopped on seeing us, we threw stones at them in order to drive them down the next creek. We were just in time to do this and return to our hiding-place when we saw, on the summit of the pass and on the other side, a number of Tibetans following the yaks we had driven away. The Tibetans passed only a couple of hundred yards below us, evidently quite unaware of our presence. They were apparently looking for our tracks, for they often stooped to examine the ground.

Later in the afternoon I went to reconnoitre down the Gyanema road, in the hope of watching, unseen, the Tibetans who passed on their way to and from Taklakot. I saw no soldiers. A strong band of brigands, driving before them thousands of sheep and yaks, was an interesting sight. The bandits rode ponies, and obeyed their leader smartly when, in a hoarse voice, and never ceasing to turn his prayer-wheel, he muttered orders. They went briskly along, women and men riding their ponies astride. The men had matchlocks and swords. Each pony carried, besides its rider, bags of food slung behind the saddle. I watched the long procession from behind rocks, and felt somewhat relieved when the last horsemen, who passed only some twenty yards from me, rode away with the rest of the caravan. I retraced my steps. Judging that this camp was not quite so safe as I had at first imagined, I proceeded, with the aid of my men, to make a rough intrenchment and to erect a wall round the platform, sheltered by the projecting rock under which we lived. These bulwarks hid us from the sight of passing Tibetans, and were serviceable as fortifications in case of a night attack. All our things were buried a short distance above our camp.

Another long, dreary day had passed. We had used our last grain of salt. Yet another day on nettles alone, and a third day and a fourth on the same diet! How sick we got of nettles! The days seemed endless as, lying on a peak above our camp, I remained hour after hour scanning with my telescope the long plateau above the Gakkon River in search of our expected messengers. Every time I saw men in the distance my heart leaped, but on focussing them with my glass they turned out to be Jogpas (bandits), or Dogpas (nomad tribes of smugglers), or travelling Humlis or Jumlis, on their way to Gyanema and Gartok. As time went on and the messengers did not put in an appearance, we began to entertain doubts as to their safety. Would they betray us and never return? Or had they been caught by the Jong Pen (the Master of the fort), and been imprisoned and tortured?

My Indian servant declined to eat any more nettles. He said it was better not to eat at all than to eat the same thing constantly. He declared he could fast for ten days, and would make up for the lack of food by sleeping.

My fortified abode was comfortable enough during the

morning when the sun shone on it. Often when the rock had absorbed a good deal of heat, it got so warm that we had to abandon it in the middle of the day, when the thermometer registered as much as 120°, 122°, and even 124°. From 1 P.M. till ten o'clock at night a bitter wind blew from the south-east and seemed to get right into our bones. So cold was this wind that the temperature suddenly dropped down to 60°, and even lower, the moment the sun disappeared behind the mountains, and continued to fall as low as 40°, 34°, and 32° during the night. One night we had a terrific gale and a snow-storm. Such was the force of the wind that our wall was blown down upon us as we slept under its shelter. The hours we had hoped to rest had to be spent in repairing the damage done.

On the following morning we were gathering nettles for our meal when we heard the distant tinkling of fast-approaching horse-bells. We quickly put out the fires, hid our things, and hastened behind our bulwarks. I seized my rifle. Chanden Sing loaded the Martini. A Shoka, who was too far off to reach our fortified abode in time, screened himself behind some rocks. In the nick of time! Half a dozen soldiers, with matchlocks to which were attached red flags, were cantering gayly up the hillside only a few yards in front of us. They were undoubtedly searching for me. They looked in every direction, but fortunately never turned their eyes toward the castle walls that concealed us. Perhaps they were expecting to see a large European tent in one of the valleys, and never dreamed that we should be where we were. We covered them well with our rifles, but we had no occasion to fire. They rode on. The sound of their horse-bells grew fainter and fainter as they disappeared on the other side of the pass. These horsemen were probably soldiers despatched by the Tarjum to guard this track. They were now on their way back to their master, satisfied that the Englishman was not to be found in that part of the country.

We named that spot "Terror Camp," for many and horrible were the experiences that befell us there. Another weary day dragged slowly to its close, and no sign of the messengers' return. Two men volunteered to go into Kardam, a settlement some miles off. There they would try to obtain food from the Tibetans. One of them had a friend at that place. He would try to buy from him sufficient provisions to enable us to go on a few days longer.

Disguised as pilgrims, a disguise not difficult to assume, for their clothes were falling to pieces owing to the rough marching we had done of late, the men started and were away the whole day. When they returned late at night they had an amusing tale to tell. Meeting a tribe of Dogpas, they had boldly entered their camp, asking to purchase food. Unfortunately the Dogpas had not sufficient for themselves, and could not spare any. Incidentally my men were informed that *Lando Plenki* (the name the Tibetans had given me) had taken a large army of men into Tibet. Great excitement prevailed at Taklakot as well as at other places, owing to the fact that the Englishman had the strange power of making himself invisible when the Tibetan soldiers were near him. He had been heard of in many places in Tibet. Soldiers had been sent in all directions to capture him. His tracks had several times been discovered and followed. Yet he could never be found. Messengers had been hastily sent out from Taklakot to Lhassa (sixteen days' journey), and to Gartok, a great market in West Tibet, asking for soldiers to assist in the capture of this strange invader, who was also said to have the power of walking on water when crossing rivers and of flying over mountains when he chose.

When I recalled our struggles and sufferings in climbing over the mountains and in crossing the streams on our journey, this account of myself given by the Tibetans, and now repeated to me, struck me as almost cruelly ironical. I was pleased that the Tibetans credited me with such supernatural powers, for it would keep them from getting too close to us.

Three more long days were spent in painful anxiety regarding the fate of our messengers. We feared that they had been captured and beheaded. We had retired in despair to our fortress. It was 10 P.M. We were worn out and ready to turn in. Our fire at the bottom of the creek was slowly dying out. Nature around us was as still and silent as death. I suddenly heard sounds of approaching steps. We listened, peeping through the narrow openings in our wall. Were these Tibetans trying to surprise us in our sleep or were they my men returning at last?

We closely watched the gorge from which the sounds

came—yes, faint sounds of voices and of footsteps. At last four staggering figures crawled cautiously into camp. We could not even then discern in the dim light whether they were our messengers or not.

"*Kuan hai?*" (Who is there?) I shouted.

"Dola!" replied a voice. We gave them a joyful and hearty greeting, but our happiness was not to last long. The men did not respond. They seemed quite exhausted and terrified. I asked them to explain the cause of their distress. Sobbing and embracing my feet, they at first declined to tell me. Grave, indeed, was the news they brought.

"Your days are numbered, sir!" at last cried Dola. "It is impossible for you to get out of this country alive! . . . They will kill you! The Jong Pen of Taklakot says he must have your head at any cost."

"Do not look so far ahead, Dola," I replied, trying to console him. "Tell me, first, how you reached Taklakot?"

"Oh, sahib, we followed your plan. We suffered much on the road. The marches were long and severe, and we had little food. We walked day and night for two days, keeping away from the track, and hiding whenever we saw any one. When we got near the Tibetan fort we saw, at the foot of the hill, a few tents of Shokas from Nepal. None of the Shokas from British Territory had been allowed to enter Tibet. A guard kept a sharp lookout day and night in order to arrest anybody entering the country from that side. Two fakirs, who were on a pilgrimage to the sacred Mansarowar Lake, unaware of the danger, had crossed over the Lippu Pass, and had proceeded down to Taklakot. They were immediately seized and accused of being you, sir, in disguise. As the Tibetans were not quite certain as to which of the two was the disguised Englishman, they severely punished both, beating them almost to death. What became of them we were unable to learn. The Tibetans afterward found out that you had entered Tibet by another pass, and soldiers have been sent in every direction to look for you.

"No sooner did we appear at Taklakot," sobbed Dola, "than we were pounced upon, knocked about, and arrested. They cross-examined us closely. We professed to be Johari traders who had run short of food, and had made for Taklakot to buy provisions. They beat us and treated us badly, until your friend Zeniram, the head village man of Chongur (in Nepal), came to our rescue and gave thirty rupees surety for us. We were then allowed to remain in his tent, guarded by Tibetan soldiers. We secretly purchased from him and packed the provisions. At night Zeniram succeeded in decoying the soldiers who were guarding us into his tent, and gave them *chökti* to drink until they became intoxicated. One by one we four succeeded in escaping with our loads. For three nights we marched steadily back, hiding during the day. Now we have returned to you, sir."

Dola paused for a minute or two.

"Sir," he continued, "we were told in Taklakot that over a thousand soldiers are searching for you everywhere. More are expected from Lhassa and Sigatz,[1] whither the

[1] Usually called "Shigatze" on English maps.

Jong Pen has hastily sent messengers. They fear you, sir, but they have orders from Lhassa to capture you at any cost. They say that you can make yourself invisible when you wish. Exorcisms are made and prayers offered daily, so that in future you may be seen and arrested. Once caught, they will have no pity on you. You will be beheaded. The Jong Pen is angry with you, owing to the defiant messages you sent him from Garbyang. He has given orders to the soldiers to bring you back dead or alive. Whoever brings your head will receive a reward of five hundred rupees."

"I had no idea my head was so valuable!" I could not help exclaiming. "I shall take great care of it in the future."

In Tibet five hundred rupees represent a large fortune. The man possessing such a sum is a rich man.

My men looked upon the whole affair as very serious.

I gave a handsome reward to the four men who had brought the provisions, but that did not prevent all my Shokas declaring that the danger was so great that they must leave me there and then. Appeals are useless on such occasions. I simply said that I should shoot any man attempting to leave camp. Having now provisions for ten days, I informed my men that we must at sunrise push on.

Sulky and grumbling, the Shokas left the fortified corner and went below to the creek. They said they preferred sleeping down there. I suspected them. I sat up watching them and listening instead of sleeping. My Indian servant rolled himself up in his blanket, and, as usual, was soon asleep. The Shokas lighted a fire, sat around it, and with their heads close together held an excited council in a half-whisper. In the heated discussion some spoke louder than they imagined. The night being particularly still, and the place well adapted for carrying sound, I overheard words which put me on the alert. I soon convinced myself that they were arranging to sell my head . . . yes . . . and to divide the money!

The men got closer together, and spoke so faintly that I could hear no more. Then they each in turn placed one hand above the other along a stick, until the end of it was reached; each man then passed it to his neighbor, who went through the same performance; a queer kind of drawing lots, common among the Shokas. Eventually the man selected by fate drew from a load a large Gourkha knife, and removed its scabbard. I well remember the moment when the men, with their faces lighted by the small flame of the flickering fire, all looked up toward my aerie. Seen from the fissure in the wall behind which I knelt, their countenances seemed distorted and ghastly. They listened to hear if we were asleep. Then all but one rolled themselves in their blankets, completely covering their heads and bodies. The one figure I could now see sat up by the fire for some time, as if thinking hard. Every now and then he turned his head up toward my fortress and listened. At last he got up and, with his feet, smothered the fire. It was a lovely night, and as soon as the reddish flame was put out the stars shone like diamonds in the deep-blue sky.

I rested the barrel of my rifle on the wall, my eyes being

fixed on the black figure down below. Stooping low, the traitor crawled step by step the few yards up to my abode, pausing to listen each time a rolling stone caused a noise. He was now only two or three yards away. He seemed to hesitate. Drawing back, and ready to spring up, I kept my eyes fixed on the top of the wall. I waited some time, but the man was in no hurry. I grew impatient.

I slowly got up, rifle in hand, and as I raised my head above the wall I found myself face to face with the man on the other side. I lost no time in placing the muzzle of my Mannlicher rifle close to his face. The surprised Shoka, dropping his knife, went down on his knees and begged my pardon. He received a good pounding with the butt of my rifle. I felt I had better ascertain that no further disturbance took place during the night. Two men attempted to crawl out of camp and desert, but I discovered them and stopped them in time. At last the sun rose, and the night ended with all its troubles and anxieties.

CHAPTER X

AMONG ENEMIES AND ROBBERS

On my last scouting journey up the hill above Terror Camp I had seen, by the aid of my telescope, the encampment of a guard of Tibetans about three miles north of us.

In the morning we dug up the main part of the baggage we had buried, and made ready to start. One of my men, named Nattoo, came forward and professed to be able to guide me directly to the Mansarowar Lake. He seemed anxious to undertake this task, saying that there would be no chance of being seen by Tibetans by the route he knew, and therefore we might march during the daytime.

Led by this man, we started up the creek. I was astonished at the willingness with which the Shokas agreed to proceed. In a short time I felt convinced that Nattoo was deliberately taking us to the spot I most wished to avoid. On my remonstrating and stopping farther progress in that direction, the Shokas mutinied, and, laying down their loads, tried to escape. Chanden Sing quickly barred their way ahead in the narrow creek. I prevented their escape from the opposite side. They had to surrender. They were all severely punished there and then. On being closely cross-examined, they confessed that they had made a plot to hand me over to the Tibetan guard, in order to escape themselves the horrors of torture by the Tibetans. This last act of treachery, coming after what had happened during the night, and from the very men to whom I had been so kind, was too much for me. I used a stick, which Chanden Sing handed me, freely on their backs and legs—Nattoo receiving the largest share of blows, because he was undoubtedly the leader of the conspiracy.

On climbing to a high point of vantage I made another discovery. Besides the guard we had to the north of us, both east and west our way was barred by Tibetan soldiers. It was not possible to get on during the day without being seen. I absolutely refused to go back south. I held a council with my men, now apparently resigned to their fate. They agreed to accompany me as far as the Maium Pass (on the road to Lhassa), which we reckoned we could reach in fifteen to eighteen marches. They further agreed to endeavor to obtain yaks and food for me, and I was then to dismiss them.

From the summit of the hill I had climbed I had taken careful bearings. At night, aided by my luminous compass, I led my men high up along the mountain range at an average elevation of 1500 feet above the Gyanema-Taklakot track.

The night was dark and stormy. We encountered much difficulty on our journey forward, owing to the slippery ground. Where it was not slippery we trod over troublesome loose stones. We could not see far ahead. Though we well knew from the angle of the slope that we were travelling along a precipice, we could not distinguish anything under us except a very bright streak far, far down below—undoubtedly the river.

I could not explain the luminosity of the water. It did not seem to come from reflection of the light of stars or the moon, because the sky was cloudy at the time. The river had a curious greenish tint, closely resembling the light produced by an electric discharge. In the more dangerous spots we had to proceed for long distances on all-fours. Even then we felt hardly safe, for we could hear the sound of the stones rolling down the steep slope, and by the length of time they took to reach the bottom we knew that we were proceeding over a precipice of extraordinary height. So difficult and painful was the walking that it took us about four hours to go some three miles. We felt so exhausted that from time to time we had to lie down and rest, shivering with cold. Our hands were bleeding from cuts caused by the sharp stones. I mustered my men. Poor Mansing, the leper, was missing. When we last spoke to him he was moaning under his load, and he constantly stumbled and fell. Two men were sent in search, but after an hour's absence they failed to discover him. Faithful Chanden Sing and the Shoka Dola were then despatched to his rescue. After another hour of anxiety the two returned, bringing the unfortunate coolie with them. The poor fellow's hands and feet were badly cut. The pain in the latter was so great that he could no more stand erect. He had fallen in a faint from exhaustion, and it was by a mere chance that in the darkness Chanden Sing stumbled against his senseless body. Apart from his life, his loss would have been a serious matter to me, as he carried my bedding and photographic cameras.

Sleet and rain commenced to fall. The cold was intense. We continued to climb steadily, Chanden Sing and I helping the poor leper along. The march soon became less difficult, as we were following a depression formed by the action of melting snows. We were sheltered from the piercing wind, which had been driving the sleet hard into our faces. We slowly covered some three more miles. During that time the storm passed away, leaving the atmosphere beautifully clear. When we reached the pass (over 17,000 feet high) a curious optical phenomenon astonished us all. The larger stars and planets, of a dazzling brilliancy, such as I had never in my life seen before, seemed to swing to and fro in the sky with rapid and sudden jerks, describing short arcs of a circle, and returning each time to their normal position. The effect was so weird that I at first believed something had gone wrong with my vision, but my companions saw the same phenomenon. More curious still was the illusion of the stars nearer the horizon disappearing and reappearing behind the mountain range. The oscillations of the heavenly bodies nearer the horizon were less rapid, but the angle of the arc described measured almost double that traced by the stars directly above our heads. The oscillations of the latter were, especially at certain moments, so rapid that the star itself, instead of having its normal appearance, formed a continuous streak of light on the deep-blue background of the sky.

This strange optical illusion, which began soon after the storm had cleared away, lasted some time. Gradually the oscillations became less violent, and stars and planets eventually resumed their normal steadiness, shining with great brilliancy and beauty.

We crossed the pass, and halted directly on the northern side of it. My followers suffered intense pain. Their feet were in a terrible condition. The minimum temperature was 12° Fahrenheit. We did not pitch our tent, and when we went to sleep there was only a blanket between us and heaven. When we woke in the morning we found the thermometer had risen to 30°. We were enveloped in thick mist, which chilled us to the marrow of our bones. I had icicles hanging from my mustache, eyelashes, and hair. My cheeks and nose were covered with a thin layer of ice, caused by the breath settling and congealing on my face.

During our night marches up and down mountain ranges of great height we naturally had many adventures and escapes. In constant storms of grit and snow we crossed range after range, travelling at night and hiding during the day, always camping at great elevations. We underwent considerable privations. I steered my men toward the Rakastal, or Devil's Lake. One day, having risen to 17,550 feet, we obtained a magnificent view of the two great sheets of water, the Lafan-cho and Mafan-cho, more commonly known to non-Tibetans under the names of Rakastal and Mansarowar lakes.

To the north of the lakes stood the magnificent Tize, the sacred Kelas Mountain, overtopping by some 2000 feet all the other snowy peaks of the Gangri chain. This chain extended roughly from north-west to south-east. From this spot we could see more distinctly than from Lama Chokten the band round the base of the mountain, which, according to legend, was formed by the rope of the Rakas (devil) trying to tear down this throne of Siva.

Tize, the great sacred peak, was of fascinating interest, owing to its peculiar shape. It resembled the giant roof of a temple. Perhaps it lacked the gracefulness of sweeping curves. Tize was angular—uncomfortably angular. Its height, the vivid color of its base, and the masses of snow that covered its slopes certainly gave it a peculiar attraction. Otherwise it struck me as being intensely unpicturesque—at least from the point from which I saw it and from which the entire face of it was visible. When clouds toned down and modified its shape, Tize appeared at its best from a painter's point of view. Under these conditions, I have thought it beautiful, especially at sunrise, with one side tinted red and yellow, and its exposed rocky mass standing majestic against a background of shiny gold. With my telescope I could plainly distinguish, especially on the east side, the defile along which the worshippers make the circuit at the base of the mountain. I was told that some pilgrims actually march round it on the snowy ledge directly over the base, just above the darker band of rock described before. On the south-west side could be seen, on the top of a lower peak, a gigantic *obo* (a pyramid of stone).

The journey round Tize usually takes three days. Some accomplish it in two days, and under favorable circumstances it has even been done in one day. It is usual for the pilgrims to say certain prayers and make sacrifices as they proceed. The more fanatical perform the journey serpentwise, lying flat on the ground at each step. Others do it on their hands and knees, and others walking backward.

Tize, or Kelas, has an elevation of 21,830 feet, and Nandiphu, west of it, 19,440 feet. North-west of the sacred mountain are visible other summits 20,460 feet, 19,970 feet, and 20,280 feet high.

While I was sketching this panorama a snow leopard bounded gracefully before us. Animal life seemed to abound. I had a shot or two at a *thar* (mountain goat), and we saw any number of *kiang* (wild horse). We found rhubarb, which seemed to be thriving at so high an elevation as 17,000 feet, and quantities of yellow flowers in the same locality and at the same elevation. At 19,000 feet I netted two couples of small white-and-black butterflies. They seemed to have great difficulty in flying.

On nearing the lakes the atmosphere seemed saturated with moisture. No sooner had the sun gone down than there was a heavy dew, which soaked our blankets and clothes. We were at 16,550 feet in a narrow, marshy creek in which we had descended precipitously from the last mountain range. From the summit of the range we had seen many columns of smoke rising from the neighborhood of the Devil's Lake. We judged that we must again proceed with great caution.

We cooked our food. In the middle of the night, for

greater safety, we shifted our camp in a north-easterly direction on the summit of the plateau. We continued our journey in the morning high above the magnificent blue sheet of the Devil's Lake with its pretty islands.

"Sir, do you see that island?" exclaimed Nattoo, pointing at a barren rock in the lake. "On it," he continued, "lives a hermit Lama, a saintly man. He has been there alone for many years, and he is held in great veneration by the Tibetans. He exists almost entirely on fish and occasional swan's eggs. Only in winter, when the lake is frozen, is communication established with the shore, and supplies of *tsamba* are brought to him. There are no boats on the Devil's Lake, nor any way of constructing rafts, owing to the absence of wood. The hermit sleeps in a cave, but generally comes out in the open to pray to Buddha."

During the following night, when everything was still, a breeze blowing from the north conveyed to us, faint and indistinct, the broken howls of the hermit.

"What is that?" I asked of the Shokas.

"It is the hermit speaking to God. Every night he climbs to the summit of the rock, and from there addresses his prayers to Buddha the Great."

"How is he clothed?" I inquired.

"In skins."

Late in the afternoon we had an amusing incident. We came to a creek in which were a number of men and women, hundreds of yaks and sheep, and some thirty ponies.

The Shokas became alarmed, and immediately pronounced the folks to be brigands. I maintained that they were not. Kachi had a theory that the only way to tell brigands from honest beings was to hear them talk. The brigands, he declared, usually shouted at the top of their voices when conversing, and used language far from select, while well-to-do Tibetans spoke gently and with refinement. I thought the only thing to do was to go and address the people, when by the tone of voice we should find out who and what they were. This, however, did not suit my Shokas. We were placed in a rather curious position. In order to proceed on our journey we must either pass through the Tibetan encampment or we must march southward round a mountain, which would involve considerable trouble, fatigue, and waste of time. We waited till night came, watching, unseen, the Tibetans below us. As is customary with them, at sundown they retired to their tents. Leaving my men behind, I crawled into their camp during the night and peeped into one of the tents. The men were squatting on the ground, round a fire in the centre, upon which steamed two vessels with stewing tea. One old man had strongly marked Mongolian features, accentuated by the heavy shadows which were cast by the light of the fire on his angular cheekbones and prominent and wrinkled brow. He was busily revolving his prayer-wheel from left to right, repeating, in a mechanical way, the usual *Omne mani padme hun*, words which come from the Sanscrit, and refer to the reincarnation of Buddha from a lotus flower, meaning literally, "O God, the gem emerging from a lotus flower." Two or three other men whose faces I could not well see, as they were stooping low, were counting money and examining several articles of Indian manufacture which undoubtedly had been seized from Shokas.

Having discovered the best way to pass without being seen, I went back to my men, and led them, in the middle of the night, through the Tibetan camp. We proceeded for a mile or so beyond the encampment. Having selected a well-sheltered spot where we thought we could rest without fear of discovery, we laid down our loads and tried to get a few hours' sleep. At sunrise we were startled on finding our camp surrounded by a band of robbers. Our friends of the previous night had followed our tracks, and, mistaking us for Shoka traders, had now come for a little pleasant robbery. On drawing near they were given a somewhat warm reception. Their instant retreat was more speedy than dignified.

We wended our way along a narrow valley toward the shore of the Devil's Lake, halting to cook our food about half a mile from the water's edge. At this point I took observations for longitude, also the correct elevation with boiling-point thermometers. Water boiled at 185° with the temperature of the atmosphere at 64° Fahrenheit.

I had just repacked my instruments, and was lying flat in the sun, some distance away from my men, when I thought I saw something move. Jumping up, I caught sight of a stalwart Tibetan stealing along the ground only a few yards away from me, with the object, no doubt, of seizing my rifle. He was not quick enough. All he got was a good pounding with the butt of my Mannlicher. I recognized him; he was one of the brigands we had seen in the morning. They had followed and spied us all along. Having got over his first surprise and begged for mercy, the bandit, with an amusing air of assumed innocence, requested us to go and spend the night in his tent with him and his friends. They would treat us right royally, he said. Being well acquainted with the hospitality of robbers, we declined the invitation. The brigand went away somewhat shaken and disappointed. We continued our journey along the edge of the Devil's Lake. Hundreds of hares sprang all around us. So numerous were they that I killed several with my rifle, using bullet cartridges. There were signs all along that at some previous epoch the level of the lake must have been much higher than it is at present.

Marching during the day, we encountered many Tibetans, some of whom were Dogpas, others Jogpas, both nomad bands of robbers. When they saw us approaching they generally fled, driving their sheep and yaks in front of them. We came upon two Tibetan women, very dirty. Their faces were smeared with black ointment, as a protection for the skin and to prevent its cracking in the high wind. They were dressed in long sheepskin garments, worn out and filthy. The shaggy hair was so unwashed that it emitted a sickening odor. I ordered them not to come too near us.

Later four Tibetans, who attempted to snatch Chanden Sing's rifle out of his hand, received from him a battering they were not likely to forget. After this we were left alone for the remainder of the day. In the evening Chanden Sing fired at a black wolf which came close to camp. I discovered, about one hundred feet above the lake-level, imbedded in the mountain-side, a stratum of gigantic fossils, which, owing to their size and weight, I was unable to dig out and carry away.

Feeling almost certain that we were being spied upon all the time by the numerous Jogpas we had met, and knowing their favorite habit of attacking strangers at night while asleep, we generally resorted to a simple ruse. Before sunset we pretended to encamp, and having lighted a fire to let them think that we had halted for the night, after dark escaped, leaving the fire burning. Walking and stumbling for several miles, we eventually found a spot high on the hillside, where we considered ourselves safe. Snow fell heavily during the night, and as usual we woke up with icicles hanging from our mustaches, eyelashes, and hair. Otherwise we really felt happy and well.

It was my good-fortune to make quite sure, from many points, that the ridge between the Rakas and Mansarowar lakes was continuous, and no visible communication between the two lakes existed. With the exception of a small depression about half-way across, the ridge has an average height of 1000 feet all along—a fact which ought in itself to dispose of the theory held by some that the two lakes are connected by a wide channel intersecting this ridge. I ascertained from the natives that there was no visible communication between the lakes, though the depression in the ridge makes it probable that at a very remote period some connection existed. The lowest point in this depression in the centre of the ridge is over three hundred feet above the level of the lakes.

CHAPTER XI

IN STRANGE COMPANY

Just before leaving the shores of the Rakastal I had a great piece of luck. We had been detected by another band of brigands, who were trying to overtake us. I had watched them with my telescope as they rode toward us. They were driving some twenty yaks in front of them at a fast pace. The brigands rode ponies. We were about a mile and a half ahead of them, and close to the edge of the Devil's Lake. We saw them coming down the hill-side at a breakneck speed straight in our direction. It was evident that they were after us. My men became terror-stricken when I gave order to halt.

The band of highwaymen approached, leaving the yaks in charge of two women. When they galloped in a line toward us, my men, with the exception of Chanden Sing and Mansing, were paralyzed with fright.

The brigands were now one hundred yards off. With loaded rifle in one hand and my camera in the other, I advanced to meet them, knowing that, with their old-fashioned matchlocks, it took them a considerable time to light the fusee and fire a shot. Moreover, it was almost an impossibility for them to fire on horseback, their weapons being heavy and cumbersome.

I focussed them in my twin-lens photographic appara-

THE BANDITS LAID DOWN THEIR ARMS

tus, and waited till I had them well in the field. I snapped the picture when they were only thirty yards away, vaulting over their ponies in the act of dismounting. The camera, having done its work, was quickly deposited on the ground, and the rifle shouldered. I shouted to them to put down their weapons. To give force to my request I aimed at them with my Mannlicher.

A meeker lot of brigands I do not believe could be found anywhere. People of that kind were only brave when it was easy for them to be courageous. The matchlocks were quickly unslung from their shoulders and flung to the ground. Their jewelled swords were laid by the side of the firearms. The bandits went down on their knees, and taking off their caps with both hands, put out their tongues in sign of salute and submission. I could not help taking another photograph of them in that comical attitude.

Chanden Sing, who had been left to look after the baggage, had placed Mansing in charge, and was now by my side with the Martini-Henry rifle, when one of the women, riding astride, arrived on the scene. She was evidently furious at the cowardice of her men. I liked her for that. She jumped off her steed, ejaculated words at the top of her voice, shaking her fists at the men still kneeling before me, and at last, foaming with rage, spat on them. While thus haranguing the band of highwaymen, she had an annoying way of pointing at my baggage; but her speech seemed to have little effect on the submissive crowd.

I went up to her, patted her on the back, and offered her

a rupee if she would hold her tongue. She grabbed the coin, and rubbed it on her skin coat to make the silver shine. She instantly became calm, and rubbing the coin until it was quite bright, she raised her fiery eyes, staring into mine, and put out her tongue to express her thanks.

Kachi and Dola, who knew Tibetan well, were now summoned to address the bandits for me; but these two Shokas were in such terror that they could hardly walk, much less speak. After a while, however, seeing how well I had these terrible people under control, they were able to translate.

"I want them to sell me some yaks and some ponies," I said. "I will pay handsomely for them."

"They say they cannot. The Tarjum will cut their heads off if he comes to know it. They will only sell one or two yaks."

"Very good. How much do they want?"

"Two hundred silver rupees. But," added Dola, "sir, do not give them more than forty. That is a great deal more than they are worth. A good yak costs from ten to sixteen rupees."

After some three or four hours' bargaining, during which time the bandits descended gradually from two hundred rupees to forty, and I rose from twenty to that figure, we at last agreed, amid the greatest excitement on both sides, that their two best yaks should be my property. Becoming quite friendly, they also sold me pack-saddles and sundry curiosities. They gave me tea and *tsamba*. The fiery woman had still a peculiar way of keeping her eyes fixed on my baggage. Her longing for my property seemed to increase when she saw me pay for the yaks and suspected that I must have a good deal of money. If she kept one eye on my goods, I kept both there. I took good care that my rifle was never out of my hand, and that no one ever came too near me from behind.

We counted the money down, some fifty rupees, including all purchases. Each coin was passed round and sounded by each of our sellers, and when the entire sum was handed over the coins were passed back and recounted, so that there should be no mistake. Time in Tibet is not money, and my readers must not be surprised when I tell them that counting, recounting, and sounding the small amount took two more hours. The two yaks were eventually handed over to us—one, a huge, long-haired black animal, restless and powerful; the other equally black, strong, and hairy, but somewhat gentler.

To catch them, separate them from the herd, pass ropes through their respective nostrils, and tie pack-saddles on their backs, were all operations we as novices had to master. It was hard work indeed, but we struggled until we succeeded.

When we parted, the brigands and I were good friends. The bandits behaved admirably. I came to the conclusion that, in Tibet, I would at any time rather deal with a bandit than with an official.

In a way I was sorry when my interview with the Jog-pas came to an end, for, although they were undoubtedly brigands, they were certainly interesting. Their original and curious dress, their manner, their conversation, their unusual but eminently sensible mode of eating, and their jovial freedom of demeanor were really quite refreshing. Their dress was quite representative of Tibet. The men wore a great variety of coats and hats, probably due to the facility with which they obtained them. No two individuals were dressed alike, though certain leading features of dress were to be observed in each case. One man wore a gaudy coat trimmed with leopard skin. Another had a long, gray woollen robe like a dressing-gown, taken up by a waist-band. A third was garbed in a loose raiment of sheepskin, with the wool inside. Yet a fourth was arrayed in a dark-red tunic fastened by a belt of leather with silver ornamentations inlaid in wrought-iron. Suspended to the belt were a needle-case, tinder-pouch and steel, a bullet-pouch and bag, and a pretty dagger with a sheath of ebony, steel, and silver filigree. In their belts the Jogpas, in common with the majority of Tibetan men, wore a sword in front. Whether the coat was long or short, it was invariably loose and made to bulge at the waist, in order that it might contain a number of eating and drinking bowls (*pu-kus*), snuff-box, sundry bags of money, *tsamba*, and bricks of tea. It was owing to this custom that most Tibetan men, when seen at first, gave the impression of being very stout, whereas, as a matter of fact, they were somewhat lightly built. In the daytime the Tibetans left one arm and part of the chest bare, letting one sleeve hang. The reason for this practice was because in Tibet the days were hot and the nights cold, the drop in the thermometer at sunset in south-west Tibet being at times as much as 80°, and even 100°. As the Tibetans always slept in their clothes, the garments that protected their bodies from being frozen at night were found too heavy and warm in the hot sun, and, therefore, that simple expedient was adopted. When sitting down both arms were drawn from the sleeves, and the chest and back were left bare; but when standing, one arm, usually the left, was slipped in, to prevent the coat and its heavy contents falling off.

That the Jogpas had good digestions was evident from the way they ate, when, having concluded the sale of the yaks, they squatted down to a hearty meal of *tsamba*, *chura* (cheese), and tea. They took from their coats their wooden and metal *pu-kus* (bowls), and quickly filled them with *tsamba*, pouring over it steaming tea mixed, as usual, with butter and salt in a churn. With their dirty fingers they stirred the mixture in the bowl until a paste was formed, which they rolled into a ball and ate. The same operation was repeated over and over again. Each time, before refilling, the bowl was licked clean by rotating the *pu-ku* round the tongue. Feeling the heat of the sun after their meal, both men and women removed some of their garments, showing ornaments of gold, silver, and copper encircling their necks.

The women of the bandits, though far from beautiful, possessed a certain charm, due entirely to their wildness. Unlike most Tibetan women, they had good teeth. Their complexion was not specially dark. Only the black ointment, with which their cheeks, noses, and foreheads were smeared, made them appear darker than they really were, and was decidedly unbecoming. They had regular features. Their eyes and mouths were full of expression. Twisted into numberless little plaits, the hair was brought up and fastened over the head. A red turban kept the plaits in position, and was raised so as to show another row of little plaits decorating the forehead. The end of each of these plaits was joined to its immediate neighbor. These ladies wore large ear-rings of gold inlaid with malachite.

The children were talkative, and acted like grown-up people. They wore swords in their belts, even at the early age of eight or ten years.

In a basket that had been carried on one of the yaks I saw an infant a few months old. His superstitious mother snatched the child away in horror when I caressed him, and washed and rubbed the poor little fellow's face until the skin was sore, declaring that children died who were touched by strangers.

The men were just as superstitious. When I wished to buy some rice from them, they would not let me handle it till it had become my property. They objected each time that I stretched out my arm to touch the bag of rice, and eventually showed me a handful of rice at a distance, to let me judge of its quality. I first bought only the handful. Having assured myself that it was good, I then purchased the remainder.

We had marched on the same afternoon about half a mile in the direction of Mansarowar, when we were overtaken by one of the brigands, whom we had left a short time before. He rode toward us, apparently in great excitement. Having dismounted, he drew his sword and began chasing one of my yaks. This seemed so strange a proceeding that we were at a loss to understand his intentions. He screamed to us that he meant no harm, so we let him go on. He eventually overtook one yak, and, after a struggle with the unfortunate animal, he flung his arms round the beast's neck and rested his head between its horns. I was getting rather anxious, fearing that this effusion was only a dodge to cut the beast's throat. Much to my astonishment, I saw that the young Jogpa had seized a tuft of the yak's hair with his teeth and was trying to tear it off, while the unfortunate quadruped was making desperate efforts to shake off its persecutor. The hair eventually gave way, and with a tuft of it hanging from his tightly closed lips, the Jogpa let go the animal's head, and, brandishing his sword, next made a dash for its tail.

I thought it was time to interfere. I seized the man by his pigtail, while he in his turn clung to the tail of the frightened yak, which, bolting, dragged both of us after it at an unpleasant pace.

The Jogpa, in our mad flight, cut off a long lock of the yak's silky hair. Having secured this, he appeared to be quite satisfied, let go, and sheathed his sword. He quickly concealed the stolen locks in his coat, and then made low bows to us, sticking out his tongue, and declaring that unless such a precaution were taken when parting with a beast, bad luck was sure to come to you. This closed the incident. The Jogpa rode away perfectly happy, and we continued our march across the stony plain until we reached the ridge which extended across it, and in its continuation divided the two lakes. We climbed up to the top, rising to 16,450 feet. In order to make certain that the ridge really extended right across between the two lakes, I made an excursion about half way along its length, and found that the northern part seemed somewhat lower than the southern; but in the portion between the two sheets of water, and barring the central depression which I have already mentioned, it seemed everywhere several hundred feet above the level of the lakes. This expedition incurred some loss of time, and when night came we were still on the ridge.

From our camping-ground we saw fifteen black tents on the hillside. To the east, on the lake shore, there was a large Gomba, or Lamasery, with a temple and a number of mud houses. I estimated the distance between ourselves and the Gomba at only eight miles, a cheering fact, because I hoped to get there fresh provisions that would enable us to proceed more rapidly on our journey. We were now quite out of reach of the Gyanema soldiers, as well as of such troublesome officials as the Barca Tarjum and the Jong Pen of Taklakot. If we could only obtain a sufficient quantity of food during the night, and proceed across country early the next day, there would be little danger of being overtaken by our pursuers. The Shokas were again shaking with fright at the idea of entering a Tibetan settlement. I told them firmly that we must reach Tucker Gomba and village that night.

We had below us the two great lakes. Before I left this magnificent panorama I could not help taking a last long look at the marvellous scene. The Devil's Lake, with its broken, precipitous shores, its rocky islands and outstretching peninsulas, was far more enchanting to me than the sacred lake by its side, in which, according to tradition, dwelled Mahadeva and all the other good gods. Although the water was equally blue and limpid, although each lake had for a background the same magnificent Gangri chain, Mansarowar, the creation of Brahma, was not nearly so weirdly fascinating as its neighbor. Mansarowar had no ravines rising precipitously from its waters. It was almost a perfect oval without indentations. There was a stony, slanting plain some two miles wide between the water's edge and the hills surrounding it, except along the ridge separating it from the Rakastal, where its coast was slightly more rugged and precipitous.

Directly south of the lake was a chain of high peaks covered with snow, from which several streams descended. From where we stood we could see evident signs, as in the case of the Rakastal, that the level of the lake must at one time have been at least thirty feet higher than it was when I visited it. The slanting bed of small, rounded, smooth stones, which extended from one and a half to two miles beyond the water-line, was evidence enough that the level of the water must have been up to that point. I believe that the lake was gradually receding.

Round the lake there were several tumbling-down sheds in charge of Lamas. Only one important Gomba (monastery) and a temple were to be seen — *viz.*, at Tucker Village.

I was told that a small Gomba and *serai* (resting-house

for pilgrims), in charge of Lamas, stood to the north-west of the lake, but I cannot vouch for the accuracy of the statement, as I did not visit it myself, and the information I received from Tibetans regarding its position and importance was conflicting.

As the nature of the country suddenly changed between the Devil's Lake and Mansarowar, so, too, the weather and the temperature greatly changed. Over the Rakastal we invariably saw a lovely blue sky, whereas over Mansarowar heavy black clouds hung overhead and rain fell incessantly. From time to time the wind blew off the rain for a few minutes, and lovely effects of light played upon the water. Fresh clouds, with violent bursts of thunder, soon made the scene again gloomy and depressing.

It was much warmer on the Mansarowar side of the ridge than on the Rakastal side. Probably owing to the dampness, the air seemed quite thick to breathe, instead of being crisp and light, as it was along the shores of the Devil's Lake. Indeed, when I recall the Mansarowar, I cannot help thinking that it was the home, not only of the gods, but also of storms.

We descended some two miles to the plain, and crossed a rapid delta of the Langa Tsangpo, or Langa River; then another, a mile farther. As these rivers came directly from the snows, the water was very cold, and often three or four feet deep, owing to the thawing of the snow and ice during the day.

CHAPTER XII

AMONG THE LAMAS

No sooner had we reached the shores of the Mansarowar than the heavy clouds, which had been hanging over our heads, poured forth such torrents of rain that in a moment we were drenched to the skin. We were marching fast, as our heavy loads were now on the two yaks. Night was well advanced. The darkness was such that we could only see a few inches in front of us. We were actually walking in an inch or two of water. A fierce south-east wind drove the rain and hail so hard into our faces and hands as to cause us considerable pain. We were chilled in our wet garments, and our teeth were chattering. We walked quickly, keeping close together. From time to time a bright flash of lightning shone on the lake, and was followed by a terrific crash of thunder. We took advantage of what we could see during those few seconds of light to steer our way toward Tucker Village and Gomba.

The rivers, swollen by the rain, were extremely difficult to cross. The water seemed to flow so rapidly on the inclined bed that it was all we could do to keep on our feet. So wet were we that we did not even take the trouble to remove our shoes and garments, and we splashed, clothes and all, across the streams we encountered. Three times we went into the freezing water above our waists, and then marched on for endless miles on the pebbly and stony incline. We could no more see where we were going. The storm seemed to grow worse every minute. We stumbled on amid large stones and bowlders, and fell over one another on slippery rocks. Farther on we sank up to our knees in mud, which stuck in lumps to our feet and made them as heavy as lead. It was a downpour such as I had seldom before experienced.

"Are you quite sure that this lake is the home of the gods?" I inquired of Kachi. "Why, even on the Devil's Lake we had better weather than this."

"Yes, sir," replied Kachi. "But you make the gods angry, and that is why they send thunder, hail, and rain to stop your progress. You are going on against the gods, sir."

"Never mind, Kachi. It cannot pour forever."

At midnight we had no idea where we were; still we pushed on.

"Have we passed the Gomba? Have we not yet reached it?" were the questions we asked one another. It seemed to me that, at the rate we were going, we should have been near the place, and yet after another hour's tramp we had not struck it. I was under the impression that we had gone about nine miles. I expressed the opinion that we had passed it, but the Shokas insisted that we had not, so we again proceeded.

We had hardly gone five hundred yards when we heard the faint, distant, and most welcome bark of a dog. It came from the north-west, and we surmised that it must come from Tucker. We had steered too far south of the place, which accounted for our missing it in the darkness.

Guided by the yelping, we hastily directed our steps toward the settlement. Suddenly the first dog was joined by fifty others, all angry and noisy; but though we knew by the sound that we were approaching the village, it was so dark and stormy that we could not find the place. Only when we found ourselves close to the mud huts could we be certain that we had at last arrived.

It was then between 2 and 3 A.M. The rain still came down in torrents. There was no sign of the inhabitants being willing to give us shelter. It was quite out of the question to pitch our little *tente d'abri*, for our things were already wringing wet.

We knocked on a door so hard that the door itself nearly gave way. This was a shelter-house, a *serai* for pilgrims, and as we claimed to be pilgrims, we had, by the laws of the country, a right to admission. Nattoo, who had once before reached this lake by a different route, led us to this house.

"You are bandits," said a hoarse voice from inside, "or you would not come at this hour."

"No, we are not," we entreated. "Please open. We are well-to-do people. We will harm no one, and pay for all."

"*Middù, Middù!*" (Cannot be, no!) "You are brigands. I will not open."

To show that we were not what they imagined, Chanden Sing and Dola tapped again so gently at the door that the bolt gave way. The next moment ten strangers were squatting down round a warm fire drying their shrivelled-up, soaked skins by the flame of dried tamarisk and dung. The landlord—a doctor, by-the-way—was re-assured when he saw that we had no evil intentions, and found some silver coins in the palm of his hand. Yet, he said, he rather wished we would go and sleep somewhere else. There was a capital empty hut next door, he suggested.

On our agreeing to this, he conducted us to the place, and there we spent the remainder of the night—or, rather, the early morning.

Our abode was a one-storied flat-roofed house built of stones and mud. There were two rooms—the first lighted by the door, the second and larger having a square opening in the ceiling for the triple purpose of ventilation, lighting, and outlet for the smoke of the fire, which burned directly underneath in the centre of the room. The beams and rafters supporting the roof had been brought over from the Indian side of the Himahlyas, as no timber was to be found in western Tibet.

This building was in charge of a young, half-crazy Lama, who was most profuse in salutations, and who remained open-mouthed, gazing at us for a considerable time. He was polite and attentive. He helped to dry our things in the morning, and, whenever we asked for anything, he ran out of the house in frantic fits of merriment, always bringing in what we required.

The heavy storm during the night had flooded our room. There was only one corner of the floor slightly drier than the rest. There we all slept huddled together. These *serais* have no claim to cleanliness. On this occasion all the minor animal life that inhabited the floor had, with a view to avoiding the water, retreated to the higher portion of the room, which we also had selected, so that one more trial was added to all our other miseries. We were simply devoured by a swarm of insects. This, indeed, was a dreadful pest, and one from which we suffered indescribable agonies, not only on this occasion, but whenever we halted near Tibetan camps.

When we rose in the morning the room was full of Tibetan men, women, and children, who seemed good-natured and friendly.

"*Tanga chick!*" (a silver coin equivalent to half a rupee) cried an old woman, who stuck a dried fish under my nose, professing volubly that it had been caught in Mansarowar, and that it would make its possessor the happiest of mortals. Others unrolled, from inside pieces of red cloth in which they were wrapped, jewellery in the form of brooches, rings, and ear-rings of brass or silver, inlaid with malachite.

"*Gurmoh sum!*" (Three rupees!), "*Diu, diu, diu!*" (Yes, yes, yes!), "*Karuga ni!*" (Two two-anna pieces!), "*Gieutcheke!*" (A four-anna piece!), and so on, they called out the price of each article, all talking at the same time, in their anxiety to dispose of their goods.

The jewellery was of local manufacture. In some cases the pieces of malachite were firmly set, but usually a kind of paste was used for holding the stones, and, consequently, pretty as the jewels were, they soon broke.

The ear-rings were usually better made than the brooches. The most interesting of all, because simpler and more characteristic, were the flat silver charms, ornamented with a primitive design.

Several Lamas came to call on me in the morning, and professed to be pleased to see us; in fact, they asked me to go and pay them a visit in the Lamasery and temple. They said there was much sickness in the village, and as they believed me to be a Hindoo doctor, they wished I could do something to relieve their sufferings. I promised to do all I could. I was glad to have this unique chance of visiting a Lamasery. During this friendly visit to the Lamas I carried my rifle in my hand. The Tibetans were too friendly to be trusted.

When I came out of our stuffy, dark room, preceded and followed by a crowd of inquisitive natives, I had a good look round the village. After the storm of the night we fully expected that the weather would clear and that we might see a bright blue sky, but we had no luck. Over us hung again threatening clouds. The waters of the sacred lake, softly moved by the wind, washed gracefully upon the beach. Chanden Sing and Mansing, the two Hindoos, without any clothing except a loincloth, were squatting near the edge of the lake having their heads shaved by Bijesing, the Johari. I must confess that I was somewhat annoyed when I saw them using my best razor for the purpose. I repressed my anger on remembering that, according to their religion, the fact of being at Mansarowar absolved them from all sins. My two Hindoo servants, with heads turned toward Kelas Mount, were praying so fervently that I stood to. watch them. They washed themselves repeatedly, and at last plunged into the water of the lake. On coming out, shivering with cold, they each took out of their clothes a silver rupee, and flung it into the lake as an offering to the God Mahadeva. Then, with hairless faces and heads, they dressed and came to pay their salaams to me, professing to be now happy and pure.

"Siva, the greatest of all gods, lives in the waters of Mansarowar!" exclaimed Chanden Sing, in a poetic mood. "I have bathed in its waters, and of its waters I have drunk. I have salaamed the great Kelas, the sight of which alone can absolve all sins of humanity. I shall now go to heaven."

"I shall be satisfied if we get as far as Lhassa," grumbled the sceptical Mansing, out of ear-reach of the Tibetans.

Chanden Sing, who was well versed in religious matters, explained that only Hindoo pilgrims who had lost both parents shaved their heads on visiting Mansarowar, as a sacrifice to Siva. If they were of a high caste, on their return to their native land after the pilgrimage it was customary to entertain all the Brahmins of the town to a banquet. According to Chanden Sing, a man who had bathed in Mansarowar was held in great respect by everybody, and commanded the admiration and envy of the entire world.

The Mansarowar Lake is about forty-six miles round. Pilgrims who wish to attain a great state of sanctity make a *kora*, or circuit, on foot along the water-line. The journey occupies from four to seven days, according to circumstances. One trip round will absolve the pilgrim from ordinary sins; twice the circuit clears the conscience of any murder; and three times will make honest and good a person who has killed his or her father, mother, brother, or sister. There are fanatics who make the tour on their knees; others accomplish the distance lying flat upon the ground after each step.

According to legend, Mansarowar was created by Brahma. He who shall bathe in its waters will share the paradise of Mahadeva! No matter what crimes he may have previously committed, a dip in the holy lake is sufficient to purge the soul as well as the body of any criminal!

When they had finished purifying themselves by washing, I ordered Chanden Sing to take his rifle and follow me into the Gomba. Having committed no crime, I thought I had better do without the holy bath, although the temptation was great to go and have a swim. The Lamas were so polite that I feared treachery on their part. To please my men and perhaps bring myself some luck, I hurled a couple of coins into the lake.

The large square building, with its walls painted red and its flattish dome of gilt copper, rose by the waterside, and was both picturesque and handsome in its severe simplicity.

There came sounds from inside of deep, hoarse voices muttering prayers, of tinkling of bells and clanging of cymbals. From time to time a drum was beaten, giving a hollow sound, and an occasional and sudden touch upon a gong caused the air to vibrate until the notes faded away as they were carried over the holy lake.

After Chanden Sing and I had entered the Lamasery, the large door, which had been pushed wide open, was immediately closed. We were in a spacious court-yard, three sides of which had two tiers of galleries supported by columns.

This was the *Lhaprang*, or Lamạ's house. Directly in front of me was the *Lha Kang*, or temple, the floor of which was raised some five feet above the level of the ground. A large door led into it. At this entrance were, one on either side, recesses in which, by the side of a big drum, squatted two Lamas with books of prayers before them, a praying-wheel and a rosary in their hands, the beads of which they shifted after every prayer. At our appearance the monks ceased their prayers and beat the drums in an excited manner. There seemed to be some disturbance in the Gomba. Lamas old and young rushed to and fro out of their rooms, while a number of *Chibbis*, or novices (boys between the ages of twelve and twenty), lined the railings of the upper veranda with expressions of evident suspense and curiosity upon their faces. No doubt the Lamas had prepared a trap for us. I warned Chanden Sing to be on the alert, and set him on guard at the entrance of the temple. I deposited a few silver coins on the drum of the Lama to my right, took off my shoes in sign of respect, and—much to the amazement of the monks—quietly entered the house of worship. Partly astonished at the sight of the silver, and more so at my want of caution, the Lamas, of whom there were a good number in the court-yard, remained motionless and dumb. The High Lama, or Father Superior of the monastery, at last came forward stooping low. He placed one thumb above the other and put his tongue out to show his approval of my visit to the many images representing deities or sanctified Buddhist heroes which were grouped along the walls of the temple. The largest of these figures were about five feet high, the others about three feet. Some were carved out of wood, their drapery and ornaments being fairly artistic in arrangement and execution, while others were fashioned in gilt metal. There were images in a sitting posture and some standing erect. They rested either on ornamented or plain pedestals painted blue, red, white, and yellow. Many wore the ancient Chinese double-winged cap, and were placed in recesses in the wall decorated with stuffs, wood-carvings, and rough paintings of images.

At the foot of these images was a long shelf, on which, in bright brass vessels of all sizes, were oblations of *tsamba*, dried fruit, *chura*, wheat, and rice, offered, through the Lamas, by devotees to the different saints. Some of the ears of barley were ornamented with imitation leaves modelled in butter, and colored red, blue, and yellow.

The ceiling of the temple was draped in red woollen cloth similar to that of the clothes worn by the Lamas. From it hung hundreds of strips of silk, wool, and cotton of all colors. The roof was supported by columns of wood forming a quadrangle in the centre of the temple. These were joined by a balustrade, compelling the worshippers to make a circuit from left to right, in order to pass before the several images.

In a shrine in the central part of the wall facing the entrance was *Urghin*, or *Kunjuk-chick* (God alone). In front of it on a kind of altar covered with a carpet were to be seen donations far more abundant than those offered to other images.

The Lama, pointing at it, told me that it was a good God. I saluted it and deposited a small offering in the collection-box. This seemed to please the Lama greatly, for he at once fetched a holy-water amphora, hung with long "veils of friendship and love,"[1] and poured some scented liquid on the palms of my hands. Then, producing a strip of veil, he wetted it with the scent and presented it to me. The majority of pilgrims generally go round the inside of the temple on their knees, but, notwithstanding that, to avoid offending prejudices, I generally follow the principle of doing in Rome as the Romans do, I could not here afford the chance of placing myself at such a disadvantage in case of a surprise. The High Lama explained the different images to me, and threw handfuls of rice over them as he called them by their respective names, all of which I tried hard to remember, but, alas! before I could get back to the *serai* and scribble them down on paper, they had all escaped my memory. A separate entrance led from the monastery into the temple.

Lights, burning in brass bowls, their wicks being fed

[1] *Kala* (veil of friendship and love)—a long piece of gauze presented on all occasions in Tibet in order to show friendly feelings.

with melted butter, were scattered on the floor in the central quadrangle. Near them lay oblong books of prayers printed on the smooth yellow Tibetan paper made from a fibrous bark. Near these books were small drums and cymbals. One double drum, I noticed, was made from reversed sections of human skulls. My attention was also attracted by some peculiar head-gear worn by the Lamas during their services and ceremonies, when they not only accompany their chanting and prayers with the beating of drums and clashing of cymbals, but they also make a noise on cane flutes, tinkle hand-bells, and sound a large gong. The noise of these instruments is at times so great that the prayers themselves cannot be heard. Awe-inspiring masks are used by Lamas in their eccentric and mystic dances. The Lamas spend the entire day in the temple and consume much tea with butter and salt in it, which is brought to them in cups by Lamas of an inferior order acting as servants. They pass hour after hour in their temples, apparently absorbed in praying to the God above all gods, the incarnation of all the saints together united in a trinity, the *Kunjuk-Sum.*

Kunjuk-Sum, translated literally, means "the three deities." Some take it to refer to the elements—air, water, and fire—which in the Tibetan mind are symbols of speech, charity, and strength or life. One great point in Buddhism is the love and respect for one's father and mother, and the prohibition to injure one's neighbors in any way. The latter is preached, but seldom practised. According to the commandments contained in some eight hundred volumes called "the Kajars," the Tibetans believe in a heaven (the *Deva Tsembo*) free from all anxieties of human existence, full of love and joy. Their heaven is ruled over by a god of infinite goodness, helped by countless disciples called the *Chanchubs*, who spend their existence in performing charitable deeds among living creatures. With a number of intermediate places of happiness and punishment, they even believe in a hell where the souls of sinners are tormented by fire and ice.

"God sees and knows everything, and He is everywhere," exclaimed the Lama, "but we cannot see Him! Only the *Chanchubs* can see and speak to Him."

"What are the evil qualities to be mostly avoided?" I inquired of the High Lama, who spoke a little Hindustani.

"Luxury, pride, and envy," he replied.

"Do you ever expect to become a saint?" I asked him.

"Yes, I hope so; but it takes five hundred transmigrations of an uncontaminated soul before one can be a saint."

Then, as if waking to a sudden thought, he seized my hand impulsively and spread my fingers apart. Having done this, he muttered two or three words of surprise. His face became serious, even solemn, and he treated me with strange obsequiousness. Rushing out of the temple, he went to inform the other Lamas of his discovery, whatever it was. They crowded round him, and from their words and gestures it was easy to see they were bewildered.

When I left the company of the strange idols and came into the court-yard, every Lama wished to examine and touch my hand. The sudden change in their behavior was to me a source of great curiosity, until I learned the real cause of it some weeks later.

CHAPTER XIII

LIFE IN THE MONASTERIES

BEFORE I left the monastery the Lamas asked me many questions about India and concerning medicine. They also questioned me as to whether I had heard that a young Englishman had crossed over the frontier with a large army, which the Jong Pen of Taklakot had defeated, beheading the leader and the principal members of the expedition.

I professed to be ignorant of these facts. I was amused at the casual way in which the Jong Pen of Taklakot had disposed of the bear-skin before he had even caught the bear. The Lamas mistook me for a Hindoo doctor, owing to the color of my face, which was sunburnt, and had long remained unwashed. I wore no disguise. They thought that I was on a pilgrimage round the Mansarowar Lake. They appeared anxious to know whether illnesses were cured by occult science in India, or by medicine only. I, who, on the other hand, was more interested in getting information than in giving it, turned the conversation on the Lamas themselves.

There are sects of red, yellow, white, and black Lamas. The red ones are the older and more numerous throughout the country. Next to them come the yellow Lamas, the *Gelupkas*, equally powerful in political and religious matters, but not quite so numerous. The white Lamas and the black Lamas, the *Julinba*, are the craftsmen in the monasteries. They do the painting, printing, pottery, and the ornamentation of temples, besides attending on the other Lamas and making themselves useful in the capacities of cooks, shepherds, water-carriers, writers, and last, but not least, executioners. The Lamaseries are usually rich. The Tibetans are a deeply devout race, and the Lamas are not backward in extorting money, under pretences of all kinds, from the ignorant worshippers. Besides attending to their religious functions, the Lamas are traders. They carry on a brisk money-lending business, charging a high interest, which falls due every month. If this should remain unpaid, all the property of the borrower is seized, and if insufficient to repay the loan the debtor himself becomes a slave of the monastery. The well-fed countenances of the Lamas are, with few exceptions, evident proof that notwithstanding their occasional bodily privations, they do not allow themselves to suffer in any way. They lead a smooth and comfortable existence of comparative luxury.

The larger Lamaseries receive a yearly Government allowance. Considerable sums are collected from offerings of the faithful, and other moneys are obtained in all sorts of ways which, in any country less religious than Tibet, would be considered dishonorable and even criminal. In Tibet it is well known that, except in the larger towns, nearly all people, excluding brigands and Lamas, are poor, while the monks and their agents thrive on the fat of the land. The masses are maintained in complete ignorance. Seldom is a layman found who can read or write.

The Lamaseries and the Lamas, as well as the land and property belonging to them, are absolutely free from all taxes and dues. Each Lama and novice is supported for life, and receives an allowance of *tsamba*, bricks of tea, and salt. The Lamas are recruited from all ranks. Honest folks, murderers, thieves, swindlers—all are eagerly welcomed in joining the brotherhood. One or two male members of each family in Tibet take monastic orders, and thus the monks obtain a powerful influence over each house or tent-hold. It is hardly an exaggeration to say that in Tibet half the members of the male population are Lamas.

In each monastery are found Lamas, Chibbis,[1] and a lower grade of ignorant and depraved Lamas—slaves, as it were, of the higher Lamas. The latter dress, and have clean-shaven heads like their superiors. They do all the handiwork of the monastery; but they are mere servants, and take no direct, active part in the politics of the Lama Government. The Chibbis are novices. They enter the Lamasery when young, and remain students for many years. They are constantly under the teaching and supervision of the older ones. Confession is practised, from inferior to superior. After undergoing successfully several examinations, a Chibbi becomes a Lama, which word translated means "high-priest." These Chibbis take minor parts in the strange religious ceremonies in which the Lamas, disguised in skins and ghast-

[1] *Chibbis*—also frequently pronounced *Chabis*.

ly masks, sing and dance with extraordinary contortions to the accompaniment of weird music of bells, horns, flutes, cymbals, and drums.

Each large monastery has at its head a Grand Lama, not to be confounded with the Dalai Lama of Lhassa, who is believed, or rather supposed, to have an immortal soul transmigrating from one body into another.

The Lamas eat, drink, and sleep together in the monastery, with the exception of the Grand Lama, who has a room to himself. For one "moon" in every twelve they observe a strict seclusion, which they devote to praying. During that time they are not allowed to speak. They fast for twenty-four hours at a time, with only water and butter-tea, eating on fast-days only sufficient food to remain alive, and depriving themselves of everything else, including snuff and spitting—the two most common habits among Tibetan men.

The Lamas have great pretensions to infallibility, and on account of this they claim, and obtain, the veneration of the people, by whom they are supported, fed, and clothed. I found the Lamas, as a rule, intelligent, but inhuman, even barbarously cruel and dishonorable. This was not my own experience alone. I heard the same from the overridden natives, who wished for nothing better than a chance to shake off their yoke.

Availing themselves of the absolute ignorance in which they succeed in keeping the people, the Lamas practise to a great extent strange arts, by which they profess to cure illnesses, discover murders and thefts, stop rivers from flowing, and bring storms about at a moment's notice. Certain ceremonies, they say, drive away the evil spirits that cause disease. The Lamas are adepts at hypnotic experiments, by which means they contrive to let the subjects under their influence see many things which are not there in reality. To this power are due the frequent reports of apparitions of Buddha, seen generally by single individuals, and the visions of demons, the accounts of which terrify the simple-minded natives. Rather than get more closely acquainted with these evil spirits the ignorant pay the monastery whatever little cash they may possess.

Mesmerism plays an important part in the weird Lama dances, which show the strangest kind of movements and attitudes. The dancer finally falls into a cataleptic state, and remains rigid, as if dead, for a long time.

The larger Lamaseries support one or more Lama sculptors, who travel to the most inaccessible spots in the district, in order to carve on cliffs, rocks, stones, or on pieces of horn, the everlasting inscription, "*Omne mani padme hun*," which one sees all over the country.

Weird and picturesque places, such as the highest points on mountain passes, gigantic bowlders, rocks near the sources of rivers, or any spot where a *mani* wall exists, are the places most generally selected by these artists upon which to engrave the magic words alluding to the reincarnation of Buddha from a lotus flower.

The prayer-wheels, those mechanical contrivances by which the Tibetans pray to their god by means of water, wind, and hand power, are also manufactured by Lama artists. The larger ones, moved by water, are constructed by the side of, or over, a stream. The huge cylinders on which the entire Tibetan prayer-book is inscribed are revolved by the flowing water. The prayers moved by wind-power are merely long strips of cloth on which prayers are often printed. As long as there is motion there is prayer, say the Tibetans, so these strips of cloth are left to flap in the wind. The small prayer-wheels, revolved by hand, are of two different kinds, and are made either of silver or copper. Those for home use are cylinders about six inches high. Inside these revolve on pivots the rolls of prayers which, by means of a projecting knob above the machine, the worshipper sets in motion. The prayers can be seen revolving inside through a square opening in the cylinder. The prayer-wheel in every-day use in Tibet is usually constructed of copper, sometimes of brass, and frequently entirely, or partly, of silver. The cylinder has two movable lids, between which the prayer-roll fits tightly. A handle with an iron rod is passed through the centre of the cylinder and roll, and is kept in its place by means of a knob. A ring, encircling the cylinder, is attached to a short hanging chain and weight. This, when started by a jerk of the hand, gives the wheel a rotatory movement, which must, according to rule, be from left to right. The words "*Omne mani padme hun,*" or simply "*Mani, mani,*" are repeated while the wheel is in motion.

The more ancient wheels have prayers written by hand instead of being printed. Charms, such as rings of malachite, jade, bone, or silver, are often attached to the weight and chain by which the rotatory movement is given to the wheel. These praying-machines are found in every Tibetan family. Every Lama possesses one. They are kept jealously, and it is difficult for strangers to purchase the genuine ones.

Besides the rosary, which is used as with the Roman Catholics, one prayer for each bead, the Lamas have a brass instrument which they twist between the palms of their hands while saying prayers. It is from two and a half to three inches long, and is rounded so as to be easilv held in the hollow of the two hands.

In Tibet, as in other Buddhist countries, there are nunneries as well as Lamaseries. The nuns, most unattractive in themselves, shave their heads, and practise witchcraft and magic, just as the Lamas do. They are looked down upon by the masses. In some of these nunneries strict confinement is actually enforced. The women of the nunneries are quite as immoral as their brethren of the Lamaseries, and at their best they are but a low type of humanity.

The only Lamas who, at certain periods of the year, are legally allowed an unusual amount of freedom with women, are those who practise the art of making musical instruments and eating-vessels out of human bones. The skull is used for making drinking-cups, *tsamba* bowls, and single and double drums. The bone of the upper arm, thigh-bone, and shin-bone are turned into trumpets and pipes. These particular Lamas are said to relish human blood, which they drink out of the cups made from men's skulls.

When I left the Gomba—my new friends, the Lamas,

bowing down to the ground as I departed—I walked about the village to examine all there was to be seen.

Along the water's edge at the east end of the village stood in a row a number of tumbling-down Choktens of mud and stone. These structures consisted of a square base surmounted by a moulding, and an upper decoration in ledges, topped by a cylindrical column. Each was supposed to contain a piece of bone, cloth, or metal, and books or parts of them, that had once belonged to a great man or a saint. Roughly drawn images were occasionally found in them. In rare cases, when cremation had been applied, the ashes were collected in a small earthenware urn and deposited in one of the Choktens. The ashes were made into a paste with clay, and then flattened into a medallion on which a representation of Buddha was either stamped from a mould or engraved with a pointed tool.

The interior of the houses at Tucker was no better than the outside. Each habitation had a walled court-yard. The top of the wall, as well as the edge of the flat roof of the house, was lined with masses of tamarisk for fuel. In the court-yard sheep and goats were penned at night. The human beings who occupied the rooms were dirty beyond all description. There were hundreds of flying-prayers over the monastery, as well as over each house. The people, laughing and chatting, stood on the roofs watching us.

While I was strolling about some fifty or sixty men armed with matchlocks and swords appeared on the scene. I looked upon them with suspicion, but Kachi reassured me, and said they were not soldiers, but a powerful band of robbers encamped about half a mile off, and on friendly terms with the Lamas. As a precaution I loaded my rifle. This was quite sufficient to cause a stampede of the armed crowd, followed, in the panic, by all the other villagers who had collected round us. Like all Tibetans, they were a miserable lot, though powerfully built and with plenty of bluster about them.

Early in the morning I had made inquiries about provisions, and had arranged for the purchase of two fat sheep and some four hundred and fifty pounds of food—flour, rice; *tsamba*, *ghur* (sweet paste), sugar, salt, and butter. Several Tibetans stated they could supply me with any quantity I required. Among others was a Shoka trader from Buddhi, who promised to bring me, within an hour, a sufficient quantity of food to last us ten men twenty-five days. I noticed, when these men left, that two of my Shokas ran after them, and entered into an excited discussion with them. Some two or three hours later the traders returned, swearing that not an ounce of food could be obtained in the place. The way in which these men could lie was marvellous. I reprimanded my Shokas, threatening to punish them severely if my suspicions of their treachery proved to be well founded.

The Shokas, finding themselves discovered, and through fear of the Tibetans, were now again demoralized. It was no use keeping them by force, and I decided to discharge them. From the moment I had entered the forbidden country I had been compelled to protect myself against them quite as much as against the Tibetans. I reflected, however, when I made up my mind to let them go, that these fellows had stood for my sake hardships and privations which few men could stand. In paying them off I therefore rewarded them suitably, and in their gratitude they undertook to bring back safely across the frontier part of my baggage containing photographs, ethnological collections, etc. This promise was duly fulfilled. With infinite trouble I then managed to purchase enough provisions to last five men ten days.

The whole party accompanied me three and a quarter miles farther, where in sight of the tumbling-down Panku Gomba, a mile to the west of us, we halted in order to make the necessary arrangements for our parting, unseen by the Tibetans. I took observations for latitude and longitude. The water of the hypsometrical apparatus boiled at 185° Fahrenheit, fifty feet above the level of the lake, the temperature of the air being 76° and the hour 10 A.M.

We could see a high snowy chain to the south of us, extending approximately from south-west to north-east, starting from the Nimo Namzil peak.

When everything was ready the five Shokas, including Kachi and Dola, left me, swearing by the sun and all that they held most sacred that they would in no way betray me to the Tibetans.

Bijesing the Johari and Nattoo agreed to accompany me as far as the Maium Pass, so that my party, including myself, now was reduced to only five men.

CHAPTER XIV

ANOTHER DISASTER

EVERYTHING promised well when, with my reduced party, I started toward the north-east, first skirting the lake for three and a quarter miles, then ascending over the barren hill ranges in an easterly direction for a distance of twelve miles. The journey was uneventful. My four men seemed in the best of spirits. We descended to a plain where water and grass could be found. Having come upon a camping-ground with a protecting wall, such as are usually put up by Tibetans at their halting-places, we made ourselves comfortable for the night, notwithstanding the high wind and a passing storm of hail and rain, which drenched us to the skin. The thermometer during the night went down to 34°.

At sunrise I started to make a reconnaissance from the top of a high hill wherefrom I could get a bird's-eye view of a great portion of the surrounding country. It was of the utmost importance for me to find out which would be the easiest way to get through the intricate succession of hills and mountains, and I also wished to ascertain the exact direction of a large river to the north of us, which discharged its waters into the Mansarowar. I started alone. A three and a half miles' climb brought me to the summit of a hill, 16,480 feet, where I was able

A NATURAL CASTLE

to ascertain all I wished to know. I returned to camp, and we proceeded on a course of 73° 30′, crossing over a pass 16,450 feet high. Then we found ourselves in front of a hill, the summit of which resembled a fortress, with flying-prayers flapping in the wind. At the foot of the hill were some twenty ponies grazing.

With the aid of my telescope I made sure that what at first appeared to be a castle was nothing but a work of nature. Apparently no one was concealed up there. The ponies, however, indicated the presence of men, and we had to proceed with caution. In fact, rounding the next hill, we discerned in the grassy valley below a number of black tents, two hundred yaks, and about a thousand sheep. We kept well out of sight behind the hill. We went a long way around it, and at last descended into an extensive valley. The river described a semicircle through this valley, close to the southern hill range, and it was joined by a tributary coming from the south-east. This tributary at first appeared to me larger than what I afterward recognized to be the main stream. I followed its course for four miles, but found that it was taking me in a more southerly direction than I wished, and had to retrace my steps along a flattish plateau.

Meeting two Tibetan women, I purchased, after endless trouble, a fat sheep out of a flock they were driving before them. These two females carried rope slings in their hands. The accuracy with which they could fling stones and hit the mark at great distances was really marvellous. For a few coppers they gave an exhibition of their skill, hitting any sheep they liked in their flock, even at distances of thirty and forty yards. I tried to obtain from these dangerous creatures a little information about the country, but they professed absolute ignorance.

"We are servants," they said, "and we know nothing. We know each sheep in our flock, and that is all. Our lord, whose slaves we are, knows all. He knows where the rivers come from, and the ways to all Gombas. He is a great king."

"And where does he live?" I inquired.

"There, two miles off, where that smoke rises to the sky."

The temptation was great to go and call on this "great king," who knew so many things. We might probably persuade him to sell us provisions. As we had none too many, they would be of great assistance to us. Anyhow the visit would be interesting. I decided to risk it.

We steered toward the several columns of smoke that rose before us, and at last we approached a large camp of black tents. Our appearance caused a commotion. Men and women rushed in and out of their tents in great excitement.

"*Jogpas! jogpas!*" (Brigands! brigands!) somebody in their camp shouted. In a moment their matchlocks were made ready, and the few men who had remained outside the tents drew their swords, holding them clumsily in their hands in a way hardly likely to terrify any one.

To be taken for brigands was a novel experience for us. The war-like array was in strange contrast to the terrified expressions on the faces of those who stood there armed. In fact, when Chanden Sing and I walked forward and encouraged them to sheathe their steels and put their matchlocks by, they readily followed our advice, and brought out rugs for us to sit upon. Having overcome their fright, they were most anxious to be pleasant.

"*Kiula gunge gozai deva labodù*" (You have nice clothes). I began the conversation, attempting flattery, to put the chieftain at his ease.

"*Lasso, leh*" (Yes, sir), answered the Tibetan, apparently astonished, and looking at his own attire with an air of comical pride.

His answer was sufficient to show me that the man considered me his superior. Had he thought me an equal or inferior he would have said *lasso* without the *leh*.

"*Kiula tuku taka zando?*" (How many children have you?) I rejoined.

"*Ni*" (Two).

"*Chuwen bogpe, tsamba, chon won ì?*" (Will you sell me flour or *tsamba*?)

"*Middù*" (Have not got any) he replied, making several quick semicircular movements with the upturned palm of his right hand.

This is a most characteristic gesture of the Tibetan, and nearly invariably accompanies the word "No," instead of a movement of the head, as with us.

"*Keran ga naddoung?*" (Where are you going?) he asked me, eagerly.

"*Nhgarang ne koroun!*" (I am a pilgrim!) "*Lungba quorghen neh jelghen*" (I go looking at sacred places).

"*Gopria zaldo. Chakzal wortzé. Tsamba middù. Bogpe middù, guram middù, dié middù, kassur middù*" (I am very poor. Please hear me. I have no *tsamba*, no flour, no sweet paste, no rice, no dried fruit).

This, of course, I knew to be untrue. I calmly said that I would remain seated where I was until food was sold to me. At the same time I produced one or two silver coins, the display of which in Tibet was always the means of hastening the transaction of business. In small handfuls, after each of which the Tibetans swore that they had not another particle to sell, I managed, with somewhat of a trial to my patience, to purchase some twenty pounds of food. The moment the money was handed over they had a quarrel among themselves about its division, and they almost came to blows. Greed and avarice are the most marked characteristics of the Tibetans. Tibetans of any rank are not ashamed to beg in the most abject manner for the smallest silver coin.

The men of the party were picturesque. They had flat, broad noses, high cheek-bones, and small, slanting (mere slits), piercing eyes. Their hair was plaited in long pig-tails ornamented with pieces of red cloth, discs of ivory, and silver coins. Nearly all wore the typical dark-red coat, with ample sleeves hanging over the hands, and pulled up at the waist to receive eating-bowls, snuff-box, and other articles of daily use. All were armed with jewelled swords.

They stood at a respectable distance, studying our faces and watching our movements with apparent interest. I have hardly ever seen such cowardice as among these big, hulking fellows. To a European it scarcely seemed conceivable. The mere raising of one's eyes was sufficient to make a man dash away frightened. With the exception of the chief, who pretended to be unafraid, notwithstanding that he was trembling with fear, they one and all showed ridiculous nervousness when I approached them to examine the ornaments they wore round their necks, such as the charm-boxes that dangled prominently on their chests. The larger of these charm-boxes contained an image of Buddha, the others were mere empty brass or silver cases.

When night came I did not consider it safe to encamp near the Tibetans. We moved away, driving our yaks before us and dragging the newly purchased sheep. We marched two and a half miles, and then halted in a depression (16,050 feet), where we had a little shelter from the wind, which blew with great force. To our right was a short range of fairly high mountains stretching from north to south. Through a gorge flowed a large stream. At that time of the evening we could not hope to cross it, but an attempt might be made in the morning, when the cold of the night would have checked the melting of the snows, and therefore lowered the level of the water in the river. Heavy showers had fallen during the day. The moment the sun went down there was a regular downpour. We had pitched our little shelter-tent, but we had to clear out of it a couple of hours later, the small basin in which we had pitched it having turned into a regular pond. There was no alternative for us but to come out into the open. Where the water did not flood us the wind was so high and the ground so moist that it was not possible to keep our tent up. The pegs would not hold. The hours of the night seemed long as we sat tightly wrapped in our waterproofs, with feet, hands, and ears almost frozen. At dawn there were no signs of the storm abating. We had not been able to light a fire in the evening, nor could we light one now. We were cold, hungry, and miserable. The thermometer had been down to 36°. Toward noon, the rain still pouring down in torrents and there being no sign of its clearing, we loaded our yaks and entered the gorge between the snow-covered mountains. With difficulty we crossed the tributary we had so far followed, and then proceeded along the right bank of the main stream.

We were so exhausted and wet that when near the evening we came to an enormous cliff, on the rocky face of which a patient Lama sculptor had engraved in huge letters the characters, *Omne mani padme hun*, we halted. The gorge was very narrow here. We found a dry spot under a big bowlder, but as there was not sufficient room for all five, the two Shokas went under the shelter of another rock a little way off. This seemed natural enough. I took care of the weapons and the scientific instruments, while the Shokas had under their own sheltering bowlder the bags containing nearly all our provisions except the reserve of tinned meats. The rain pelted all night, the wind howled. Again we could not light a fire. The thermometer did not descend below 38°, but the cold, owing to our drenched condition, seemed intense. In fact, we were so chilled that we did not venture to eat. Crouching in the small dry space at our disposal and without tasting food, we eventually fell fast asleep. I

CAMP WITH GIGANTIC INSCRIPTIONS

slept soundly for the first time since I had been in Tibet. It was broad daylight when I woke up.

Taking advantage of the storm, the men Nattoo and Bijesing had escaped during the night with the loads intrusted to them. I discovered their tracks, half washed away, in the direction from which we had come the previous night. The rascals had bolted, and there would have been comparatively little harm in that, if only they had not taken with them all the stock of provisions for my two Hindoo servants, and a quantity of good rope, straps, and other articles, which we were bound to miss at every turn, and which we had absolutely no means of replacing.

Of thirty picked servants who had started with me, twenty-eight had now abandoned me. Only two remained faithful: Chanden Sing and Mansing the leper!

The weather continued horrible. No food for my men and no fuel! I proposed to the two Hindoos to go back also and let me continue alone. I described to them the dangers of following me farther, and warned them fully, but they absolutely refused to leave me.

"Sir, we are not Shokas," were their words. "If you die, we will die with you. We fear not death. We are sorry to see you suffer, sir, but never mind us. We are only poor people, therefore it is of no consequence."

This last disaster should, I suppose, have deterred us from further progress. It somehow made me even more determined to persist than before. It was no light job to have to run afield to capture the yaks, which had wandered off in search of grass; and having found them and driven them back to our primitive camping-place, to tie upon their backs the pack-saddles, and fasten on them the heavy tin-lined cases of scientific instruments and photographic plates. This task was only part of the day's work, which included the writing up of my diary, the registering of observations, sketching, photographing, changing plates in cameras, occasionally developing negatives, surveying, cleaning rifles, revolver, etc. The effort of lifting up the heavy cases on to the pack-saddles was, owing to our exhausted condition, a severe tax on our strength. The tantalizing restlessness of the yaks forced us to make many attempts before we actually succeeded in properly fastening the loads, particularly as the Shoka deserters had stolen our best pieces of rope and the leather straps. One of the remaining pieces of rope was hardly long enough to make the final knot to one of the girths. Neither Chanden Sing nor Mansing had sufficient strength to pull and make it join. I made them hold the yak by the horns to keep him steady while I pulled my hardest. I succeeded with a great effort, and was about to get up when a terrific blow from the yak's horn struck me in the skull an inch behind my right ear and sent me rolling head over heels. I was stunned for several moments. I gradually recovered, but the back of my head was swollen and sore for many days after.

We proceeded along the right bank of the river between reddish hills and distant high snowy mountains to the north-west and east-south-east of us, which we saw from time to time when the rain ceased and the sky cleared.

The momentary lifting of the clouds was ever followed by another downpour. Marching became unpleasant and difficult, sinking, as we were, deep in the mud. Toward evening we suddenly discovered some hundred and fifty soldiers riding full gallop in pursuit of us along the river valley. We pushed on, and having got out of their sight behind a hill, we changed our course and rapidly climbed up to the top of the hill range. My two men with the yaks concealed themselves on the other side. I remained lying flat on the top of the hill, spying with my telescope the movements of our pursuers. They rode unsuspectingly on, the tinkling of their horse-bells sounding pleasant to the ear in that deserted spot. Thinking that we had continued our way along the river, they rode beyond the spot where we had left the path. Owing to their haste to catch us up, they did not notice our tracks up the hill-side.

Rain began to fall heavily again, and we remained encamped at 17,000 feet, with our loads ready for flight at any moment. The night was spent none too comfortably. I sat up all night, rifle in hand, in case of a surprise, and I was indeed glad when morning came. The rain had stopped, but we were now enveloped in a white mist which chilled us. I was tired. Chanden Sing was intrusted to keep a sharp watch while I tried to sleep.

"*Hazur, hazur, jaldi apka banduk!*" (Sir, sir, quick, your rifle!) muttered my servant, rousing me. "Do you hear the sound of bells?"

The tinkling was quite plain. Our pursuers were approaching, evidently in strong force. There was no time to be lost. To successfully evade them appeared impossible. I decided to meet them rather than attempt flight. Chanden Sing and I were armed with our rifles, Mansing with his Gourkha knife. We awaited their arrival. There came out of the mist a long procession of gray, phantom-like figures, each one leading a pony. The advance-guard stopped from time to time to examine the ground; having discovered our footprints only partially washed away by the rain, they were following them up. Seeing us at last on the top of the hill, they halted. There was a commotion among them. They held an excited consultation. Some of them unslung their matchlocks, others drew their swords, while we sat on a rock above and watched them attentively.

After hesitating a little, four officers signalled to us that they wished to approach.

"You are a great king," shouted one at the top of his voice, "and we want to lay these presents at your feet." He pointed to some small bags which the other three men were carrying. "*Gelbo! Chakzal! Chakzal!*" (We salute you, king!)

I felt anything but regal after the wretched night we had spent, but I wished to treat the natives with due deference and politeness whenever it was possible.

I said that four men might approach, but the bulk of the party must withdraw to a spot about two hundred yards away. This they immediately did—a matter of some surprise to me after the war-like attitude they had assumed at first. They laid their matchlocks down in the humblest of fashions, and duly replaced their swords in their sheaths. The four officers approached, and when quite close to us, threw the bags on the ground and opened them to show us the contents. There was *tsamba*, flour, *chura* (a kind of cheese), *guram* (sweet paste), butter, and dried fruit. The officers were most profuse in their salutations. They had removed their caps and thrown them on the ground, and they kept their tongues sticking out of their mouths until I begged them to draw them in. They professed to be the subordinates of the Tokchim Tarjum, who had despatched them to inquire after my health, and who wished me to look upon him as my best friend. Well aware of the difficulties we must encounter in travelling through such an inhospitable country, the Tarjum, they said, wished me to accept the gifts they now laid before me. With these they handed me a *kata*, or "the scarf of love and friendship," a long piece of thin silk-like gauze, the end of which had been cut into a fringe. In Tibet these *katas* accompany every gift. A caller is expected instantly on arrival to produce a *kata* for presentation to his host. The High Lamas sell *katas* to devotees. One of these scarves is presented to those who leave a satisfactory offering after visiting a Lamasery. If a verbal message is sent to a friend, a *kata* is sent with it. Among officials and Lamas small pieces of this silk gauze are enclosed even in letters. Not to give or send a *kata* to an honored visitor is considered a breach of good manners, and is equivalent to a slight.

I hastened to express my thanks for the Tarjum's kindness, and I handed the messengers a sum in silver of three times the value of the articles presented. The men seemed pleasant and friendly, and we chatted for some time. Much to my annoyance, poor Mansing, bewildered at the sight of so much food, could no longer resist the pangs of hunger. Caring little for the breach of etiquette and likely consequences, he proceeded to fill his mouth with handfuls of flour, cheese, and butter. This led the Tibetans to suspect that we must be starving, and with their usual shrewdness they determined to take advantage of our condition.

"The Tarjum," said the oldest of the messengers, "wishes you to come back and be his guest. He will feed you and your men, and you will then go back to your country."

"Thank you," I replied; "we do not want the Tarjum's food, nor do we wish to go back. I am greatly obliged for his kindness, but we will continue our journey."

"Then," angrily said a young and powerful Tibetan, "if you continue your journey, we will take back our gifts."

"And your *kata!*" I rejoined, flinging first the large ball of butter into his chest, and after it the small bags of flour, *tsamba,* cheese, fruit, etc., a minute earlier prettily laid out before us.

This unexpected bombardment quite upset the Tibetans, who, with powdered coats, hair, and faces, scampered away as best they could. Chanden Sing, always as quick as lightning when it was a case of hitting, pounded away with the butt of his rifle at the roundest part of one ambassador's body, when in his clumsy clothes he attempted to get up and run.

Mansing, the philosopher of our party, interrupted in his feed, but undisturbed by what was going on, picked up the fruit and cheese and pieces of butter scattered all over the ground, mumbling that it was a shame to throw away good food in such a reckless fashion.

The soldiers, who had been watching attentively from a distance the different phases of the interview, considered it prudent to beat a hasty retreat. Mounting their steeds with unmistakable despatch, they galloped in confusion down the hill, and then along the valley of the river, until they were lost to sight in the mist. The ambassadors, who had been unable to rejoin their ponies, followed on foot as quickly as possible under the circumstances, with due allowance for the rarefied air and rough ground.

Their cries of distress, caused by fear alone, for we had done them no real harm, served to strengthen the contempt in which my men by now held the Tibetan soldiers and their officers.

The scene was truly comical. We laughed heartily.

When the Tibetans were out of sight, Chanden Sing and I pocketed our pride and helped Mansing to collect the dried dates, apricots, the pieces of *chura*, butter, and *guram*. Then, having loaded our yaks, we marched on.

CHAPTER XV

FOLLOWED BY TIBETAN SOLDIERS

We were not in luck. The weather continued squally in the morning, and in the afternoon the rain was again torrential. We went over uninteresting and monotonous gray country. A chain of snowy peaks stretched from south-west to north-east. We waded through a fairly deep and cold river, and afterward climbed over a pass 17,450 feet high. A number of Tibetans with flocks of several thousand sheep came in sight, but we avoided them. They did not see us.

At the point where we crossed it, the main stream described a graceful bend. We climbed over undulating and barren country to an elevation of 17,550 feet, where we found several small lakelets. Having marched that day fourteen and a half miles in a drenching rain, we descended into a large valley. Here we had great difficulty in finding a spot where to rest for the night. The plain was simply a swamp, with several lakes and ponds, and we sank everywhere in mud and water. All our bedding and clothes were soaked to such an extent that it really made no difference where we halted, so we pitched our little tent on the bank of a stream intersecting a valley to the north. Extending in an easterly direction along the valley rose a series of mountains shaped like pyramids,

TORRENTIAL RAIN

covered with snow and all of almost equal height. To the south were high peaks with great quantities of snow upon them. The valley in which we camped was at an elevation of 17,450 feet. The cold was intense.

At night the rain came down in bucketfuls, and our *tente d'abri* gave us but little shelter. We were lying in water. All the trenches in the world could not have kept the water from streaming into our tent. In fact, it is no exaggeration to say that the whole valley was a sheet of water varying from one to several inches deep. Of course, we suffered intensely from cold, the thermometer dropping to 26° at 8 P.M., when a south-east wind began to blow furiously. Rain fell, mixed with sleet, for a time, and was followed by a heavy snow-storm. We lay crouched up on the top of our baggage, so as not to lie on the frozen water. When we woke in the morning our tent had half collapsed, owing to the weight of snow upon it. During the day the temperature went up and rain fell afresh, so that when we resumed our marching we sank in a mixture of mud, snow, and water several inches deep. We had to cross three rivers and to skirt five lakes of various sizes.

Seven miles of this dreary marching saw us encamped (17,380 feet) at the foot of a conical hill 17,500 feet high, where an almost identical repetition of the previous night's experience took place. The thermometer was down at 32°, but fortunately the wind subsided at eight o'clock in the evening. As luck would have it, the sun came out the following day, and we were able to spread out all our things to dry. We had yet another novel experience.

Our two yaks had disappeared. I climbed up to the summit of the hill above camp, and with my telescope scoured the plain. The two animals were some distance off, being led away by ten or twelve men on horseback, who drove in front of them a flock of about five hundred sheep. By their clothing I recognized the strangers to be robbers. Naturally I started at once to recover my property, leaving Chanden Sing and Mansing in charge of our camp. I caught them up as they were marching slowly, though, when they perceived me, they hastened on, trying to get away. I shouted three times to them to stop, but they paid no heed to my words. I unslung my rifle, and would have fired at them had the threat alone not been sufficient to make them reflect. They halted. When I got near enough I claimed my two yaks back. They refused to give them up. They said they were twelve men, and were not afraid of one. Dismounted from their ponies, they seemed ready to attack me.

As I saw them take out flint and steel in order to light the fusees of their matchlocks, I thought I might as well have my innings first. Before they could guess my intention, I applied a violent blow with the muzzle of my rifle on the stomach of the man nearest to me. He collapsed, while I administered another blow in the right temple of another man who held his matchlock between his legs, and was on the point of striking his flint and steel in order to set the tinder on fire. He, too, staggered and fell clumsily.

"*Chakzal, chakzal! Chakzal wortzïe!*" (We salute

you, we salute you! Please listen!) exclaimed a third brigand, with an expression of dismay, and holding up his thumbs with his fist closed in sign of surrender.

"*Chakzal!*" (I salute you!) I replied, inserting a cartridge into the Mannlicher rifle.

"*Middù, middù!*" (No, no!) they entreated, promptly laying down their weapons.

I purchased from these men about thirty pounds of *tsamba* and eight pounds of butter. I got one of them to carry the stuff to my camp, while I, without further trouble, recovered my yaks and drove them back to where Chanden Sing and Mansing were busy lighting a fire to make some tea.

Toward noon, when our things had got almost dry in the warm sun, the sky became clouded, and again it began to rain heavily. I was rather doubtful as to whether I should go over a pass some miles off to the east, or should follow the course of the river and skirt the foot of the mountains. We saw a large number of Tibetans travelling in the opposite direction to ours. They all seemed terrified when we approached them. We obtained from them a few more pounds of food, but they refused to sell us any sheep, of which they had thousands. I decided to attempt the first-mentioned route. Making our way first over a continuation of the flat plateau, then over undulating ground, we came to two lakelets at the foot of the pass before us. The ascent was comparatively easy, over snow. We followed the river, which descended from the pass. About half-way up, on looking back, we saw eight soldiers galloping toward us. We waited for them. As soon as they came up to us they went through the usual servile salutations, depositing their weapons on the ground to show that they had no intention of fighting. A long, amiable conversation followed, the Tibetans professing their friendship for us and their willingness to help us to get on in any way they could. This was rather too good to be true. I suspected treachery, all the more so when they pressed and entreated us to go back to their tents, where they wished to entertain us as their highly honored guests. They would shower upon us all the luxuries that human mind could conceive. These luxuries were found to consist of presents of *chura*, cheese, butter, yak milk, and *tsamba.* They said they would sell us ponies if we required them. The description was too glowing. Taking all things into consideration, and allowing for the inaccuracy of speech of Tibetans in general, I thanked them from the bottom of my heart, and answered that I preferred to continue my journey and bear my present sufferings.

They perceived that I was not easy to catch. If anything, they respected me for it. In fact, they could not conceal their amazement at my having got so far into their country with only two men. After giving my visitors some little presents, we parted in a friendly manner.

We climbed up to the pass (18,480 feet). Before us, on the other side, some two thousand feet lower, was a large stretch of flat land. I could see a lake, which I took to be the Gunkyo. To make certain of it, I left my men and yaks on the pass and went to reconnoitre from a peak 19,000 feet high north-east of us. There was much snow. The ascent was difficult and tedious. When I got to the top another high peak barred the view in front of me, so, descending first and then ascending again, I climbed this second summit, finally reaching an elevation of 20,000 feet, and obtaining a good bird's-eye view of the country all round. There was a long snowy range to the north, and directly under it what I imagined to be a stretch of water, judging from the mist and clouds forming directly above it and from the grass on the lower slopes of the mountains.

A hill range stood in my way, just high enough to conceal the lake behind it. I rejoined my men. Sinking in deep, soft snow, we continued our march down the other side of the pass. We pitched our tent at a place about five hundred feet higher than the plain below us, where the mountain sides were close together and formed a gorge. Notwithstanding that I was now quite accustomed to great elevations, the ascent to 20,000 feet had caused a certain exhaustion, and I should have been glad of a good night's rest.

Mansing and Chanden Sing, having eaten some food, slept soundly, but I felt depressed. I had a peculiar sense of unrest and a presentiment that some misfortune would come to us during the night.

We were all three under our little tent when I fancied there was some one outside. I did not know why the thought entered my head, for I heard no noise, but all the same I felt I must see for myself and satisfy my curiosity. I peeped out of the tent with my rifle in hand, and saw a number of black figures cautiously crawling toward us. In a moment I was outside on my bare feet, running toward them and shouting at the top of my voice, "*Pila tedan tedang!*" (Look out, look out!) which caused a stampede among our ghost-like visitors. There were, apparently, many of them hidden behind rocks, for when the panic seized them the number of runaways was double or even treble that of the phantoms I had at first seen approaching. At one moment there seemed to be black ghosts springing out from everywhere, only, more solid than ghosts, they made a loud noise with their heavy boots as they ran in confusion down the steep incline and through the gorge. They turned sharply round the hill at the bottom and disappeared.

When I crawled inside the tent again Chanden Sing and Mansing, wrapped head and all in their blankets, were still snoring!

Naturally I passed a sleepless night after that, fearing the unwelcome visitors might return. We speculated as to how the Tibetans had found us, and we could not help surmising that our friends of the previous afternoon must have put them on our track. However, such was the inconceivable cowardice shown on every occasion by the Tibetans, that we got to attach no importance to these incidents. Indeed, the natives did not inspire us with fear. Their visits had even ceased to excite or interest us.

We went on as usual, descending to the plain. When we had got half-way across it I scoured the hills all round with my telescope to see if I could discern traces of our pursuers.

"There they are!" cried Chanden Sing, who had the most wonderful eyesight of any man I have known. He pointed at the summit of a hill where, among the rocks, several heads could be seen peeping. We went on without taking notice of them. Then they came out of their hiding-place, and we saw them descending the hill in a long line, leading their ponies. On reaching the plain they mounted their steeds and came full gallop our way. They were quite a picturesque sight in their dark-red coats, or brown and yellow skin robes and their vari-colored caps. Some wore bright-red coats with gold braiding, and Chinese caps. These were officers. The soldiers' matchlocks, to the props of which red or white flags were attached, gave an additional touch of color to the otherwise dreary scenery of barren hills and snow. The tinkling of the horse-bells enlivened the monotony of these silent, inhospitable regions. The Tibetans dismounted some three hundred yards from us. One old man, throwing aside his matchlock and sword, walked unsteadily toward us. We received him kindly. He afforded us great amusement, for he was a strange character.

"I am only a messenger," he hastened to state, "and therefore do not pour your anger upon me if I speak to you. I only convey the words of my officers, who do not dare to come for fear of being injured. News has been received at Lhassa, from whence we have come, that a *Plenki* (an Englishman) with many men is in Tibet, and can be found nowhere. We have been sent to capture him. Are you one of his advance-guard?"

"No," I replied, dryly. "I suppose that you have taken several months to come from Lhassa." I added, pretending ignorance.

"Oh no! Our ponies are good," he answered, "and we have come quickly."

"*Chik, ni, sum, shi, nga, do, diu, ghieh, gu, chu, chuck chick, chuck ni,*" the Tibetan counted up to twelve, frowning and keeping his head inclined to the right, as if to collect his thoughts, at the same time holding up his hand, with the thumb folded against the palm, and turning down a finger as he called each number. The thumbs are never used in counting. "*Lum chuck ni niman*" (Twelve days), said he, "have we been on the road. We have orders not to return till we have captured the *Plenki*. And you," asked he, inquisitively—"how long have you taken to come from Ladak?"

He said he could see by my face that I was a native of Kashmere. I was probably so burnt and dirty that it was hard to distinguish me from a native. The old man cross-examined me to find out whether I was a native surveyor sent by the Indian Government to survey the country, and asked me why I had discarded my native clothes for *Plenki* (European) ones. He over and over again inquired whether I was not one of the *Plenki's* party.

"*Keran ga naddo ung?*" (Where are you going?) he queried.

"*Nhgarang ne koroun Lama jehlhuong*" (I am a pilgrim, going to visit monasteries).

"*Keran mi japodu*" (You are a good man).

He offered to show me the way to the Gunkyo Lake, and was so pressing that I accepted. When I saw the two hundred soldiers mount and follow us, I remonstrated with him, saying that if we were to be friends we did not need an army to escort us.

"If you are our friend, you can come alone, and we will not injure you," I gave him to understand. "But if you are our enemy, we will fight you and your army here at once, and we will save you the trouble of coming any farther."

The Tibetan, confused and hesitating, went to confabulate with his men, and returned some time after with eight of them, while the bulk of his force galloped away in the opposite direction.

We went across the plain until we came to a hill range, which we crossed over a pass 17,450 feet high. Then, altering our course, we descended and ascended several hills, and at last found ourselves in the sheltered grassy valley of the large Gunkyo Lake, extending from south-east to north-west. With a temperature of 68° Fahrenheit the water in the hypsometrical apparatus boiled at 183° 3½′ at 8.30 in the evening. The lake was of extraordinary beauty, with the high snowy Gangri mountains rising almost sheer from its waters. On the southern side lofty hills formed a background wild and picturesque, but barren and desolate beyond words. At the other end of the lake, to the north-west, were lower mountains skirting the water.

We encamped at 16,455 feet. The Tibetan soldiers pitched their tent some fifty yards away.

During the evening the Tibetans came to my camp and made themselves useful. They helped us to get fuel, and brewed tea for me in Tibetan fashion. They professed to hate the Lamas, the rulers of the country, to whom they took special pleasure in applying names hardly repeatable in these pages. According to them, the Lamas took all the money that came into the country, and no one else was allowed to have any. They were unscrupulous, cruel, and unjust. Every man in Tibet, they said, was a soldier in case of necessity, and every one a servant of the Lamas. The soldiers of the regular army received a quantity of *tsamba*, bricks of tea and butter, but no money. Usually they were provided with ponies to ride. When travelling on duty they had a right to obtain relays of animals at post-stations and villages, and they were also entitled to claim supplies of food, saddles, or anything else they required, to carry them as far as the next encampment. The weapons (sword and matchlock) generally belonged to the men themselves, but occasionally, in the larger towns, such as Lhassa and Sigatz, the Lamas provided them. Gunpowder and bullets were supplied by the authorities. The weapons were manufactured mostly in Lhassa and Sigatz. Although the Tibetans boasted of great accuracy in shooting with their matchlocks, which had wooden rests in order to allow the marksman to take a steady aim, I never saw even the champion shots of the country hit the mark. For sporting purposes and for economy's sake, the Tibetan soldiers hardly ever used lead bullets or shot, but preferred to fill the barrels of their matchlocks with pebbles. Gunpowder was so scarce that they seldom practised firing at a target.

At sunrise the view of Gunkyo was magnificent, with the snow-covered mountains tinted gold and red, and reflected in their smallest detail in the still waters of the lake.

We loaded our yaks, the Tibetans giving us a helping hand, and started toward the Maium Pass, following a river which throws itself into the Gunkyo Lake.

The valley was narrow, and with many sharp turns. Although the elevation was great, there was abundance of grass. The green was quite refreshing to the eyes, tired as we were of snow and reddish barren mountains and desert like stretches of land. We came to a basin where, on the opposite bank of the stream, was a large Tibetan camping-ground with a high wall of stones. Behind it I could see smoke rising, which made me suspect that there were people concealed.

Our Tibetan friends asked what were our intentions, and begged me to stop to talk and drink tea. I said I had had quite enough of both, and would proceed.

"If you go on we will kill you!" shouted one soldier, getting into a temper, and taking advantage of our politeness toward him and his companions.

"*Nga samgi ganta indah*" (If you please), I answered, with studied courtesy.

"If you go another step we will cut off your head, or you will have to cut off ours!" cried two or three others, stretching their bare necks toward me.

"*Taptih middù*" (I have not got a small knife), I replied, quite seriously, and with assumed disappointment, twirling my hand in the air in Tibetan fashion.

The Tibetans did not know what to make of me. When I moved toward the pass, on which hundreds of flying-prayers flapped in the wind, I politely bade them good-bye with tongue out, and waving both my hands, palms upward, in front of my forehead in the most approved Tibetan style. The soldiers took off their caps and humbly saluted us by going down on their knees and putting their heads close to the ground.

We crossed the plain, and slowly wended our way up the pass. Near the top we came to a track, the highway from Ladak to Lhassa *via* Gartok, along the northern side of the Rakastal, Mansarowar, and Gunkyo lakes. On the pass itself were planted several poles connected by ropes, from which flying-prayers waved gayly in the breeze. *Obos*, or mounds of stones, had been erected. The slabs used in the construction of these *obos* were mostly white, and bore in many instances the inscription "*Omne mani padme hun.*" Yak, goat, and sheep skulls were laid by the side of the *obos*, the above four words being engraved on the bone, and stained red with the blood of the animals killed.

Sacrifices are offered by Tibetans when crossing a high pass, especially if there is a Lama close at hand to commemorate the event. The meat of the animal killed is eaten by the people present. If the party is a large one, dancing and singing follow the feast. *Obos* are found all over the country, generally on passes or summits of hills. No Tibetan ever goes by one of these *obos* without depositing on it a white stone.

CHAPTER XVI

FIRST WHITE MAN IN THE SACRED PROVINCE

THE Maium Pass (17,500 feet), as far as which no white man had ever penetrated, is a great landmark in Tibet. Not only does one of the sources of the great Tsangpu, or Brahmaputra River, rise on its south-east slopes, but it also separates the immense provinces of Nari-Khorsum (extending west of the Maium Pass and comprising the mountainous and lake region as far as Ladak) from the Yutzang, the central province of Tibet, stretching east of the pass along the valley of the Brahmaputra and having Lhassa for its capital. The word *yu* in Tibetan means "middle." It is applied to this province because it occupies the centre of Tibet. To the north of the Maium lies the Doktol province.

I had taken a reconnoitring trip to another pass to the north-east of us, and had just returned to my men on the Maium Pass, when several of the Tibetan soldiers we had left behind rode up toward us. We waited for them. Their leader, pointing at the valley beyond the pass, cried: "That yonder is the Lhassa territory, and we forbid you to enter it!"

I took no notice of his protest, and driving before me the two yaks, I stepped into the most sacred of all the sacred provinces—"the ground of God," as they call it.

We descended quickly on the eastern side of the pass, while the soldiers, aghast, remained watching us. They were a picturesque sight as they stood among the *obos* against the sky-line, the sunlight shining on their jewelled swords and the gay red flags of their matchlocks. Above their heads strings of flying-prayers waved in the wind. Having watched us for a little while, they disappeared.

A little rivulet, hardly six inches wide, descended among stones in the centre of the valley we were following, and was soon swollen by other rivulets from melting snows of the mountains on either side. This was one source[1] of the great Brahmaputra, one of the largest rivers in the world. I must confess that I felt somewhat proud to be the first white man who had ever reached these sources, and there was a certain childish delight in standing over this sacred stream, which, of such immense width lower down, could here be spanned by a man standing with legs slightly apart. We drank of its waters at the spot where it had its birth, and then, following a marked track to the south-east, we continued our descent on a gentle incline along a grassy valley.

The change in the climate between the west and south-east sides of the Maium Pass was extraordinary. On the western side we had nothing but violent storms of hail, rain, and snow, the dampness in the air rendering the atmosphere cold even during the day. The soil was unusually marshy, and little fuel or grass could be found. The moment the pass was crossed we were in a mild,

[1] I visited the other source of the Brahmaputra River on the return journey.

pleasant climate, with a lovely deep-blue sky over us. We found plenty of grass for our yaks and low shrubs for our fires. After all our sufferings and privations, we felt that we had indeed entered the land of God. I expected great trouble sooner or later, but I was not sorry I had disobeyed the soldiers' orders and had marched straight into the most forbidden province of the forbidden land.

There is always satisfaction in doing what is forbidden.

The Brahmaputra received three small snow-fed tributaries descending from the steep mountains on either side of us. Where the main stream turned sharply south, a fourth and important tributary, carrying a large volume of water, came down through a gorge from the north-north-east.

We encamped near the junction of these rivers, on the right bank of the main stream, at an elevation of 16,620 feet. From the Maium Pass a continuation of the Gangri chain of mountains stretched first in a south-easterly direction, then due east, in a line almost parallel to the higher southern range of the Himahlyas. Between these two ranges was an extensive plain intersected by the Brahmaputra. On the southern side of the river were minor hill ranges between the river course and the big range of majestic snowy peaks. Although no peaks of considerable elevation were to be found along the range north of the Brahmaputra, yet it was of geographical importance, as its southern slopes formed the northern watershed of the holy river as far as Lhassa.

The valley enclosed between these two parallel ranges was the most thickly populated part of Tibet. Grass was abundant, and fuel easily obtainable. Thousands of yaks, sheep, and goats could be seen grazing near the many Tibetan camps along the Brahmaputra and its principal tributaries. The trade route of caravans from Ladak to Lhassa followed this valley. As I had come to Tibet to see and study the Tibetans, I thought that, although I might run greater risks, I could in no part of the country accomplish my object better than by going along this thickly populated track.

We slept little. We expected the soldiers to attack us during the night to try and stop our progress, but all was quiet and nothing happened. Our yaks got loose, and we had difficulty in recovering them in the morning. They had swum across the stream, and had gone about a mile on the other side.

The night had been very cold, the thermometer dropping as low as 32½°. We did not pitch our little tent, as we wanted to be ready in case of attack. We were tired and cold after the long march of the previous day. There was a south-westerly breeze blowing. It was hard work to have to cross the river, chase the yaks and bring them back to camp; then, exhausted as we were, to get the loads on them.

We followed the stream on the right bank. It wound in and out between barren hills, afterward flowing through a grassy valley three-quarters of a mile wide and a mile and a half long. It then went through a narrow passage and farther through an undulating grassy valley two miles wide. We were caught in a terrific thunder-storm, with hail and rain. This was an annoying experience. We were now before a large tributary of the Brahmaputra. The stream was so swollen, rapid, and deep that I was much puzzled as to how I could take my men across. They could not swim, and the water was so cold that a plunge in it would give a severe shock. There was no time to be lost. The river was visibly rising, and as the storm was getting worse, difficulties would increase every moment. We took off our clothes and fastened them, with our rifles, etc., on the pack-saddles of the yaks, which we sent into the water. These animals were good swimmers. The current carried them more than a hundred yards down-stream, but to our satisfaction they scrambled out of the water on to the opposite bank. Notwithstanding the faith that Chanden Sing and Mansing had in my swimming, they really thought their last hour had come when I took each by the hand and led them into the stream. We had hardly gone twelve yards, with water up to our necks, when the inevitable took place. We were all three swept away. Chanden Sing and Mansing, in their panic, clung tight to my arms and dragged me under water. I swam my hardest with my legs. We came to the surface several times and then sank again, owing to the dead weight of my helpless companions. At last, after a desperate struggle, the current washed us on the opposite bank, where we hastily scrambled out of the treacherous river. We were some two hundred yards down-stream from the spot at which we had entered the river, and such was the quantity of muddy water we had swallowed that we all three became sick. This left us much exhausted. As the storm showed no signs of abating, we encamped, at an elevation of 16,320 feet, there and then on the left bank of the stream. Though we sadly needed warm food, there was no possibility of lighting a fire in such torrential rain. A piece of chocolate was all I ate that night. My men preferred to eat nothing rather than break their caste by eating food prepared by European hands.

We were asleep under our little tent, the hour being about eleven, when there was a noise outside as of voices and people stumbling against stones. I was out in a moment with my rifle, and shouted the usual "*Paladò!*" (Go away!) I could see nothing, owing to the darkness, but several stones flung from slings whizzed past me. One of these hit the tent. A dog barked furiously. I fired a shot, which had the good effect of producing a hasty retreat of our enemies. The dog remained barking all night. In the morning, when I gave him food and caressed him in Tibetan fashion, with the usual words of endearment, "*Chochu, chochu,*" he rubbed himself against my legs as if he had known me all his life, and eventually lay down by the side of Mansing, to whom he took a particular fancy. From that day the dog never left our camp, and followed us everywhere until harder times came upon us.

The river was turning too much toward the south. I decided to abandon it and strike across country, especially as there were faint signs of a track leading over a pass to the east-south-east of our camp. I followed this track. Along it I detected marks of hundreds of ponies' hoofs, now almost entirely washed away. This was evidently the way taken by the soldiers we had met on the other side of the Maium Pass.

Having risen over the pass, 17,750 feet high, we saw before us an extensive valley with barren hills scattered upon it. To the south we observed a large plain some ten miles wide, with snowy peaks rising on the farther side. In front was a hill and a *mani* wall. This latter discovery made me feel quite confident that I was on the highroad to Lhassa. About eight miles off to the north-north-west were high snowy peaks, and as we went farther we discovered a lofty mountain range, with still higher peaks, three miles behind it. We had travelled half-way across the waterless plain when we noticed a number of soldiers' heads and matchlocks popping in and out from behind a distant hill. After a while they came out in numbers to observe our movements, then retired again behind the hill. We proceeded. When we were still half a mile from them they abandoned their hiding-place and galloped away before us, raising clouds of dust. From a hill 16,200 feet high, over which the track crossed, we perceived a group of very high snowy peaks about eight miles distant. Between them and us stood a range of hills cut by a valley, along which flowed a river carrying a large volume of water. This we followed, and crossed it at a suitable fording-place where the stream was twenty-five yards across. The water reached up to our waists. We found here another *mani* wall with large inscriptions on stones. As the wind was high and cutting, we used the wall as a shelter for the night. We could see in the distance the snowy Himahlyan chain. Lower hill ranges were not more than three miles from camp. The river we had just crossed flowed into the Brahmaputra. We were at an elevation of 15,700 feet. We saw plainly at sunset a number of black tents before us. We counted about sixty, and we calculated them to be two miles distant. Near them were hundreds of black yaks.

At sunrise the next morning, much to our surprise, the tents and yaks had vanished; nor, on marching in the direction where we had seen them the previous night, were we able to find traces of them. It must have been an effect of mirage. Some fourteen miles away, in a grassy plain at the foot of the range extending from north-west to south-east, and with lofty snowy peaks in a direction of 72° (bearings magnetic), we came upon a very large Tibetan encampment of over eighty black tents. We were then at an elevation of 15,650 feet. The tents were pitched on the banks of another tributary of the Brahmaputra, which, after describing a wide curve in the plain, passed west of the encampment. To the north-west, north, and north-east stood the chain of mountains which I had observed all along. The elevation of its peaks became gradually lower and lower, so much so that the name of "hill range" would be more appropriate to it than that of "mountain chain," that is to say, if the elevation of the plateau on which it stood were not taken into account. Behind it, however, towered loftier peaks with snowy caps.

We needed food, and so made boldly for the encampment. Our approach caused a commotion. Yaks and sheep were hastily driven away before us, while men and women rushed in and out of their tents, apparently in a state of great excitement. Eight or ten men reluctantly came forward, and entreated us to go inside a large tent. They said they wished to speak to us, and offered us tea. I would not accept their invitation, distrusting them, but went on across the encampment, halting some three hundred yards beyond. Chanden Sing and I proceeded afterward on a round of calls at all the tents, trying to purchase food, and also to show that, if we had declined to enter a particular tent, it was not on account of fear, but because we did not want to be caught in a trap. Our visit to the different *golingchos* or *gurr* (tents) was interesting enough. The tents themselves were cleverly constructed, and admirably adapted to the country in which they were used. The tents, black in color, were woven of yaks' hair, the natural greasiness of which made the cloth quite waterproof. They consisted of two separate pieces of thick material, supported by two poles at each end. There was an oblong aperture above in the upper part of the tent, through which the smoke escaped. The base of the larger tents was six-sided. The roof, at a height of six or seven feet above the ground, was kept tightly stretched by means of long ropes passing over high forked poles and the ends of which were pegged to the ground. Many wooden and iron pegs were required to keep the bottom of the tent close to the ground all round, so as to protect its inmates from the cutting winds of the great plateau. Outside each tent stood four long poles with white flying-prayers—one for each point of the compass. Around the interior of the larger tents there was a wall from two to three feet high for protection against the wind, rain, and snow. These walls were constructed of dried dung, which, as time went on, was used as fuel. There were two apertures, one at either end of the tent. The one facing the wind was always kept closed by means of loops and wooden bolts.

The Tibetan is a born nomad, and shifts his dwelling with the seasons, wherever he can find grazing for his yaks and sheep. He knows how to make himself comfortable. For instance, in the centre of his tent he makes himself a *goling*, or fireplace of mud and stone, some three feet high, four or five feet long by one and a half wide, with two, three, or more side ventilators and draught-holes. By this ingenious contrivance he manages to increase the combustion of the dried dung, the most trying fuel from which to get a flame. On the top of this stove a suitable place is made to fit the several *raksangs* (large brass pots and bowls), in which the brick tea, duly pounded first in a stone or wooden mortar, is boiled and stirred with a long brass spoon. A portable iron stand is generally to be seen somewhere in the tent, upon which the hot vessels are placed when they are removed from the fire. Close to these is the *toxzum* or *dongbo*, a cylindrical wooden churn, used for mixing the tea with butter and salt.

The wooden cups or bowls used by the Tibetans are called *puku*, *fruh*, or *cariel*. In them *tsamba* is eaten after tea has been poured on it, and the mixture worked into a paste by more or less dirty fingers. Lumps of butter are mixed with this paste, and even bits of *chura* (cheese). The richer people (officials) indulge in flour and rice, which they import from India and China, and in *kassur*, or dried fruit (dates and apricots) of inferior quality. The rice is boiled into a kind of soup called the *tupka*, a luxury only indulged in on grand occasions, when such other cherished delicacies as *gimakara* (sugar) and *shelkara* (lump white sugar) are also eaten. The Tibetans are fond of meat, but few can afford to eat it. Wild game, yak, and sheep are considered excellent food. The meat and bones are boiled in a cauldron with lavish quantities of salt and pepper.

The inhabitants of this encampment were polite and talkative, but I was suspicious of their friendliness. They refused to sell us food, on the plea that they had none even for themselves.

Women and men formed a ring round us. I was particularly struck, not only in this encampment but in all others, by the small number of women to be seen in Tibet. This is not because they are kept in seclusion. On the contrary, the ladies of the Forbidden Land seem to have it all their own way. They are actually in a minority, the proportion being, at a rough guess, backed by the wise words of a friendly Lama, from fifteen to twenty males to each female in the population. All the same, the fair sex in Tibet manages to rule the male majority, playing constantly into the hands of the Lamas.

The Tibetan female, whether she be a lady, a shepherdess, or a brigandess, cannot be said to be prepossessing. In fact, it was not my luck to see a single good-looking woman in the country, although I naturally saw women who were less ugly than others. With the accumulated filth that from birth is undisturbed by soap, scrubbing, or bathing; with nose, cheeks, and forehead smeared with black ointment to prevent the skin cracking in the wind; and with the unpleasant odor that emanates from never-changed clothes, the Tibetan woman is, at her best, repulsive to a European. After one has overcome one's first disgust, she yet has, at a distance, a certain charm of her own. She walks well, for she is accustomed to carry heavy weights on her head. Her skull would be well-set upon her shoulders were it not that the neck is too short and thick to be graceful. Her body and limbs possess great muscular strength, and are well developed, but generally lack firmness. She is heavily built, and inclined to stoutness.

The Tibetan woman is superior to the Tibetan man. She possesses a better heart, more pluck, and a finer character than he. Time after time, when the men, timid beyond all conception, ran away at our approach, the women remained in charge of the tents, and, although by no means cool or collected, they rarely failed to meet us without some show of dignity.

In the Tibetan encampment, when all were friendly, the women seemed less shy than the men, and conversed freely and incessantly. They even prevailed upon their masters to sell us a little *tsamba* and butter.

When a Tibetan young man wishes to marry, he goes, accompanied by his father and mother, to the tent of the lady of his heart. There he is received by her relations, who have been previously notified of the intended call,

TIBETAN WOMEN AND CHILDREN

and are found seated on rugs and mats awaiting the arrival of their guests.

After the usual courtesies and salutations, the young man's father asks, on behalf of his son, for the young lady's hand. If the answer is favorable, the suitor places a square lump of yak butter on his betrothed's forehead. She does the same for him, and the marriage ceremony is over, the buttered couple being man and wife.

Where there is a temple close by, *katas*, food, and money are laid before the images of Buddha and saints, and the parties walk round the inside of the temple. Where there is no temple, the husband and wife make the circuit of the nearest hill, or, in default of a hill, of a tent, always moving from left to right. This ceremony is repeated with prayers and sacrifices every day for a fortnight, during which time libations of wine and general feasting continue. After that the husband conveys his better half to his own tent.

CHAPTER XVII

DISASTER AT THE RIVER

COMING out of our tent in the morning, we noticed a commotion among the Tibetans. A number of mounted men with matchlocks had arrived. Others similarly armed joined them. They seemed excited. I kept my eye on them while I was cooking my food. There were some two hundred men in all, picturesquely garbed. They were good horsemen, and looked well as they rode in a line toward us. A little way off they stopped and dismounted. The leaders came forward, one stalwart fellow in a handsome sheepskin coat marching ahead of the rest. His attitude was arrogant. Dispensing with the usual salutations, he approached quite close, shaking his fist at me.

"*Kiu mahla lokhna nga rah luck tiba tangan*" (I will give you a goat or a sheep if you will go back), he said.

"*Kiu donna nga di tangon!*" (And I give you this to make you go back!) was my quick answer, while I unexpectedly administered him one straight from the shoulder that sent him sprawling on the ground.

The army, which, with its usual prudence, was watching events from a respectful distance, beat a hasty retreat. The officer scrambled away, screaming. The Tibetans had so far behaved with such contemptible cowardice that we could hardly congratulate ourselves on such easy successes. We began to feel that really we had no enemy at all before us. We became even careless. We ate our food, and gave this affair but little thought.

The Tibetans did not trouble us again that day. Those who had not ridden off retired timidly inside their black tents. Not a soul was to be seen about in the encampment. I registered my daily observations, made a sketch of one of the black tents, and wrote up my diary. Then we continued our journey.

Our progress was now comparatively easy, along a broad grassy plain. We proceeded in a south-easterly direction, observing a high snowy peak at 20° (b.m.), and a low pass in the mountain range to our north-east. A high range stood ahead of us in the far distance. At the foot of a lonely hill we found an important *mani* wall of great length, with numberless inscriptions of all ages and sizes on stones, pieces of bone, skulls, and horns. Farther on, to the south, there were three small hillocks and two larger ones. The soldiers we had routed at the encampment had proceeded in the direction we were now following. We were, in fact, treading all along on the footmarks of their ponies.

We had to cross a river and a number of rivulets. So troublesome was it each time to take off our shoes and clothes in order to wade through, that we bundled up our clothes on the yaks, and travelled along for the rest of the afternoon barefooted and with nothing on but a loincloth, in the style adopted by fakirs.[1]

[1] Religious fanatics.

The sun was extremely hot, the ground marshy, the air thick with huge and troublesome mosquitoes. We were quickly covered from head to foot with bites, which caused intense irritation. Halting on the right bank of a large stream at 15,600 feet, we named this spot "Mosquito Camp." At sunset swarms of mosquitoes made us very miserable, but fortunately the moment the sun disappeared the thermometer fell to 33°, the mosquitoes vanished, and we had a peaceful night.

In the evening we saw a number of horsemen riding full speed on a course about one mile south of ours. No doubt they were sent to keep the authorities ahead informed of our movements.

The next day the water of the stream was so clear that we could not resist the temptation of having a good cleaning up, washing first our clothes and spreading them to dry in the sun, then cleansing our faces and bodies thoroughly with soap, a luxury unknown to us for ever so long.

While—for lack of towels—I was drying myself in the sun, I admired the scenery around us. I registered at 211° (b.m.) a very high snowy peak, and a lower one at 213° 30′ forming part of a beautiful mountain chain. There were mountains on every side of the plain. Another very high peak, of which I had taken bearings on a previous occasion, was at 20° (b.m.). A break occurred in the hill range to our north-east, showing a narrow valley, beyond which were high snowy mountains. We made a long march along the grassy plain, and encamped on the bank of the Brahmaputra, there a wide, deep, and rapid stream. We saw hundreds of *kiang* and antelopes. Shortly before sunset I took a walk toward the hills to try and bring back fresh meat to camp. I stalked a herd of antelopes. When some five miles from camp I was benighted, and on my return in the darkness had the greatest difficulty in finding my men. They had been unable to light a fire, and as they had both gone fast asleep, I received no answer to my calls. We had selected a sheltered hollow in the ground for our camp, and as there were hundreds of similar depressions everywhere round it, and no landmarks to guide me, it was not easy to identify the exact place.

Fortunately, at last, after I had shouted for some considerable time, Chanden Sing heard me. By the sound of his voice, I found my way back. In the morning we noticed a large encampment about a mile off, on the opposite bank of the Brahmaputra. The stream was too rapid for us to cross, or we might have gone over to try and obtain provisions from the natives. Moreover, on further examination, we saw black tents in every direction on our side of the water, and therefore there was no reason to go to the extra trouble and danger of crossing the stream.

Much to our delight, we succeeded in purchasing a goat from some passing Tibetans, who drove before them a flock of several thousand. We could not find sufficient dry fuel to make a fire, so we intrusted Mansing with the animal as far as our next camp, where we proposed to indulge in a feast.

The Brahmaputra had here several ramifications, mostly ending in lakelets, and rendering the plain a regular swamp. The larger arm of the river was wide and deep, and we preferred following it to crossing it, notwithstanding that we had to deviate somewhat from the course which otherwise I should have followed. For several miles we sank in mud and slush up to our knees, or waded through water. There were small patches of soft earth with tufts of grass which rose above the water, but they collapsed on our attempting to stand upon them.

The whole of the northern part of the plain was extremely marshy. Our yaks gave us no end of trouble. When they sank unexpectedly in soft mud-holes, they became alarmed, and, in their struggle to save themselves, once or twice shook off their pack-saddles and loads, which we had not been able to fasten properly for want of proper ropes. Chanden Sing and I managed to keep up with the restless animals. At last, on nearing the hills, the ground showed undulations, and was rather drier. We saw columns of smoke rising from near the foot of the range to the north of us. We went on another two miles, exhausted and dirty, our clothes, on which we had spent so much soap and time in washing, filthy again with splashes of mud.

"Where are Mansing and the goat?" I asked the Hindoo.

"He remained behind at the beginning of the swamp. He was too exhausted to drag along the goat you purchased."

I was much concerned, on scouring from a hillock the country all round with my telescope, to perceive no sign whatever of the poor fellow. I was angry with myself for not noticing his disappearance before. As there were many Tibetans about the spot where he had remained, I feared foul play on their part, and that he might have been overpowered. Again I imagined that, weak as he was, he might have been sucked down in one of the deeper mud-holes, without a chance of saving himself. I left Chanden Sing to look after the yaks, and turned back in search of him. As I hurried back mile after mile, struggling again half across the mud swamp, and yet saw no trace of the poor coolie, I was almost giving up my quest in despair, when my eye caught sight of something moving about half a mile farther on. It was the goat, all alone. I made for it with a sinking heart.

It was only on getting quite close that I perceived the poor coolie, quite insensible in a faint, lying flat and half sunk in the mud. Fortunately he had taken the precaution of tying the rope to which the goat was fastened tight round his arm. To it only was due my discovering Mansing's whereabouts, not to speak of the rescue of our precious acquisition. With some rubbing and shaking I brought the poor fellow back to life, and helped him along until we rejoined Chanden Sing. Not until the middle of the night did we reach Tarbar, a large Tibetan encampment at the foot of the hill range.

The alarm of our arrival, given first by scores of dogs barking at us, then by one of the natives who had ventured peeping out of his tent to find out the cause of the disturbance, created the usual panic in the place.

"*Gigri duk! gigri duk! Jogpu, Jogpa!*" (Danger! danger! Help, brigands, brigands!) cried the Tibetan, running frantically out of his tent. A few seconds later black figures could be seen everywhere, dashing in and out of their tents. It must be remembered that, according to the manners of Tibet, one should time one's arrival at an encampment so as to reach it before sundown, unless notice of one's approach is sent ahead. People who arrive unexpectedly in the middle of the night are never credited with good motives—nothing short of murder, robbery, or extortion. I tried to set the minds of the Tibetans at ease by telling them that I meant no harm, but such was their excitement and fright that I could get no one to listen to me.

Two old women came to us with a bucket of milk and laid it at my feet, entreating me to spare their lives. Great was their astonishment when, instead of finding themselves murdered, they received a silver rupee in payment. This was the first step toward a peaceful settlement of the disturbance. After some time calm was restored, and though still regarded with suspicion, we were politely treated by the natives.

Unfortunately, here too we were unable to purchase provisions, the natives declaring that they had not sufficient food for themselves. At night the thermometer fell to 26°. We felt the cold intensely. We purchased a quantity of dung from the natives and made a fire in the morning. Having feasted on the goat, which we killed, and on yak's milk, we made preparations to strike camp early next morning. Having had a good meal after several days' privations, we felt happier than usual.

DISASTER AT THE RIVER

On leaving Tarbar we followed for a while the course of the river. It was a glorious day, and we were able to admire the magnificent panorama of the great rugged mountain range to the south-west of us. The higher peaks were nearly all shaped like pyramids. I observed a gigantic quadrangular peak which I took to be Mount Everest. Next to it was another pyramidical peak, also very lofty, but not so high and beautiful as its neighbor. I followed a general course toward east-south-east. As the river, which we had more or less followed, now described a big bend toward the south-south-east, I decided to cross it. We waded through it successfully with water up to our necks, and again we found ourselves upon marshy land, with a repetition of the previous day's experience.

Farther on we crossed three more tributaries of the larger stream, all fairly wide and deep. Then we had once more to get across the main river, there of considerable depth and swiftness. The river traversed the plain in zigzag fashion, and, unless we wanted to follow its banks, and so lengthen the journey by double or treble the distance, this was the only course open to us. Thus, while trying to travel as much as possible in a straight line, we found ourselves for the third time before this great river, now swollen by other snow-fed streams, and carrying an immense body of water. It was in the afternoon, too, when the water was at its highest. We attempted a crossing at several points, but found it impossible. I decided to wait for low water early next morning.

Apparently my yaks knew this part of the country well. I noticed that, whenever I lost the track, all I had to do was to follow them, and they would bring me back to it again. When I drove them away from the track, they showed a great disinclination to move, whereas they proceeded willingly enough while we were on the highway. No track was visible except here and there, where the footmarks of the last nomads, with their sheep, ponies, and yaks, had destroyed the grass.

Half a mile on the other side of the river was an encampment of some fifty or sixty tents, with hundreds of yaks and sheep grazing near it.

At this point my two yaks, which I noticed had been marching with more than usual smartness, bolted while I was ordering Chanden Sing and Mansing to take down the loads, and went straight into the water.

In attempting to make them turn back, Mansing threw a stone at them, which, instead of having the desired effect, sent them on all the faster. The current was strong, and the bottom of the river so soft that they both sank. When they reappeared on the surface it was only to float rapidly away down-stream. We watched them with ever-increasing anxiety. They seemed quite helpless. We ran panting along the river-bank, urging them on with shouts in order to drive them to the other side. In their desperate struggle to keep afloat, and powerless against the current, the two yaks collided violently in mid-stream. The bump caused the pack-saddle and load of the smaller yak to turn over. The animal, thus overbalanced and hampered, sank and reappeared two or three times, struggling for air and life. It was, indeed, a terrible moment. In order to save the load, I threw off my clothes and jumped into the water. I swam fast to the animal, and, with no small exertion, pulled him on shore, some two hundred yards farther down-stream. We were both safe, though breathless; but, alas! the ropes that held the baggage had given way, and saddle and load had disappeared. This loss was a dreadful blow to me. I tried hard, by repeatedly diving into the river until I was almost frozen, to recover my goods, but failed to find them or even to locate them. Where I suspected them to be the water was over twenty feet deep. The bottom of the river was of soft mud, so that the weight alone of the loads would cause them to sink and be covered over.

Diving at such great elevations gave a peculiar and unpleasant sensation. The moment I was entirely under water, I felt as if I were compressed under an appalling weight which seemed to crush me. Had the liquid above and around me been a mass of lead instead of water, it could not have felt heavier. The sensation was especially noticeable in my head, which felt as if my skull were being screwed inside a vise. The beating in my temples was almost unbearable. Under ordinary circumstances I can remain under water for over a minute, but at such high elevations I could never hold out for longer than fifteen or twenty seconds. Each time that I emerged from below, gasping for air, my heart beat alarmingly violently, and my lungs seemed as if about to burst.

I was so exhausted that I did not feel equal to conveying my two men across. I unloaded the stronger yak, and then, with endless trouble, I drove him and his mate again into the water. Unhampered, and good swimmers as they are, the two yaks floated away with the current and reached the other side. Chanden Sing and Mansing, with their clothes and mine tied into a bundle over their shoulders, got on the animals, and, after a somewhat anxious passage, arrived safely on my side. We encamped. My men mourned all night over the lost property. The next morning I made fresh and unsuccessful attempts to recover the loads. Unhappily they contained all my tinned provisions, and what little other food I had, 800 rupees in silver, the greater part of my ammunition, changes of clothing, shoes, my hurricane lantern, and sundry knives, razors, etc.

The only thing we recovered was the wooden pack-saddle, which was washed ashore some six hundred yards farther down.

Our situation can be summed up in a few words. We were now in the centre of Tibet, with no food of any kind, no clothes to speak of, and no boots or shoes, except those we wore, which were falling to pieces. What little ammunition I had left could not be relied upon, owing to its having been in water on several occasions. Around us we had nothing but enemies—insignificant enemies, if you like, yet enemies after all.

I got some comfort in thinking that the water-tight cases with my scientific instruments, notes, sketches, maps, and a quantity of gold and silver money were saved. As far as I was concerned, I valued them more than anything else I possessed.

We went on, hungry, worn out, with our feet lacerated, cheering one another as best we could. We laughed at our troubles. We laughed at the Tibetans and their comical ways. We laughed at everything and everybody, until eventually we laughed at ourselves. But the days seemed long. Though fasting gives you at first an acute pain in your inside, it does not become unbearable until after several days' absolute want of food. That is to say, if you are accustomed, as we were, to long intervals between one meal and the next. When we got to our third day's fasting we were keen enough for a meal. Perceiving black tents close to the mountain-side, about four miles out of our course, we made for them with famished haste. We purchased two bucketfuls of yak's milk, one of which I drank there and then myself, the second being equally divided between my two servants. That was all we could get. They would sell us nothing else.

After this we moved forward again, making steady, and, if one allows for the great elevation, comparatively rapid progress. We held our own against all comers. We encountered pleasant people and unpleasant ones, but, whether their manner was courteous or the reverse, we could nowhere obtain food for love or money.

Poor Mansing and Chanden Sing, not having the same interest that I had in my work to keep up their spirits, were now in a dreadful condition. Cold, tired, and starved, the poor wretches had hardly strength left to stand on their feet, the soles of which were badly cut and sore. It really made my heart bleed to see these two brave men suffer as they did for my sake. No word of complaint came from them; not once did their lips utter a reproach.

"Never mind if we suffer or even die," said the poor fellows, when I expressed my sympathy with them, "we will follow you as long as we have strength to move. We will stand by you, no matter what happens."

I had to relieve Chanden Sing of his rifle, as he was no longer able to carry it. I, too, felt languid as the days went by, and we got scarcely any food. I cannot say that I experienced severe physical pain. This was due, I think, to the fact that my exhaustion brought on fever. I had a peculiar feeling in my head, as if my intellect, never too bright, had now been altogether dulled. My hearing, too, became less acute. I felt my strength slowly dying down like the flame of a lamp with no more oil in it. The nervous excitement and strain alone kept me alive. I went on walking mechanically.

We reached an encampment of some eighty black tents and a mud guard-house. We were positively in a starved condition. It was utterly impossible to proceed farther, owing to the wretched condition of my two men. They begged to be given ponies to ride. Their feet were so sore that, notwithstanding their anxiety to follow me, they could no more.

The natives received us kindly, and consented to sell me ponies, clothes, and provisions. We encamped about two miles beyond the settlement. During the evening several persons visited my tent, bringing gifts of flour, butter, and *tsamba*, accompanied by *katas*, the veils of friendship. I made a point of invariably giving the Tibetans, in return for their gifts, silver money to an amount three or four times the value of the articles they presented us with. They professed to be very grateful. A man called Ando, who styled himself a Gourkha, but wore the garb of the Tibetans, came to visit us in our tent, and promised to bring several ponies for sale the next morning. He also undertook to sell a sufficient quantity of food to enable us to reach Lhassa. To show his good faith, he brought a portion of the supplies in the evening, and said he would let us have the remainder the next morning.

We next had a visit from a Lama, who appeared civil and intelligent. He presented us with butter and *chura* (cheese). He had travelled as far as Calcutta in India, and was then on his way from Gartok to Lhassa. Having an excellent pony, he expected to arrive there in four or five days. Other Lamas and men who came to see us stated that they had come from Lhassa in four days.

The natives, as usual, showed great reticence in giving us the name of the encampment, some calling it Toxem, others Taddju. North of us was a low pass in the hill range. As I had already seen as much as I wanted of the Tibetans, it was my intention, if I succeeded in purchasing enough provisions and ponies, to cross over this pass and proceed toward the Sacred City, following a course on the northern side of the mountain range. The highway to Lhassa was getting so thickly populated that I thought it advisable in the future to travel through less inhabited regions. I intended proceeding, dressed as a European, until within a few miles of Lhassa. Then I would leave my two men concealed in some secluded spot, and assuming a disguise, I would penetrate alone during the night into the city. This would have been easy enough, as Lhassa has no gates, and only a ruined wall round it.

I was able to purchase some clothing and boots from the Tibetans. The pigtail that I needed in order to pass for a Tibetan I could make with the silky hair of my yaks. I would pretend to be deaf and dumb, as I could not speak the Tibetan language perfectly enough to pass for a native.

A good meal brought hope and high spirits. When I retired to sleep I saw myself already inside the Sacred City walls.

CHAPTER XVIII

CAPTURED

In the night I heard noises several times. I went out of my tent to look for the disturbers, but failed to discover any one. This had become my nightly experience, and I attached little importance to these sounds.

In the morning Ando and two or three Tibetans came to sell us provisions and ponies. While my two servants and I were engaged in purchasing what we required, I saw a number of villagers approaching in groups. Some spun wool, others carried bags of *tsamba* and flour, while others led a number of ponies. Having purchased provisions to last us a couple of months, we began the selection of mounts. Naturally my servants and myself were overjoyed at our unexpected luck, after sufferings and privations of all kinds, in finding ourselves confronted with abundance of everything we could possibly desire. Chanden Sing and Mansing, who were sportsmen of the very first order, delighted at the prospect of getting animals, rode first one pony and then another to suit themselves. Chanden Sing, having selected a handsome beast, called me to examine it before paying over the purchase-money. Unsuspecting of foul play, and also because it would not have been convenient to try the various lively ponies with my rifle slung over my shoulder, I walked unarmed to the spot, about a hundred yards away from my tent, where the restless animal was being held for my inspection. The natives followed behind me, but such a thing being common in any country when one buys a horse in public, I thought nothing of it. As I stood with my hands behind my back, I well recollect the expression of delight on Chanden Sing's face when I approved of his choice. As is generally the case on such occasions, the people collected in a crowd behind me expressed in a chorus their gratuitous opinion on the superiority of the steed selected. I had just stooped to examine the pony's fore legs when I was suddenly seized from behind by several persons, who grabbed me by the neck, wrists, and legs, and threw me down on my face. I struggled and fought until I shook off some of my assailants and regained my feet; but others rushed up, and I was surrounded by some thirty men, who attacked me from every side. They clung to me with all their might, and succeeded in grabbing again my arms, legs, and head. Exhausted as I was, they knocked me down three more times, but each time I regained my feet. I fought to the bitter end with my fists, feet, head, and teeth. Each time I got one hand or leg free from their clutches, I hit right and left at any part where I could disable my opponents. Their timidity, even when in such overwhelming numbers, was indeed beyond description. It was entirely due to it, and not to my strength, for I had hardly any left, that I was able to hold my own against them for some twenty minutes. My clothes were torn in the fight. Long ropes were thrown at me from every side. I became so entangled in them

PURCHASING PONIES

that my movements were impeded. One rope which they flung and successfully twisted round my neck completed their victory. They pulled hard at it from the two ends, and while I panted and gasped with the exertion of fighting, they tugged and tugged in order to strangle me. I felt as if my eyes would shoot out of my head. I was suffocating. My sight became dim. I was in their power. Dragged down to the ground, they stamped, and kicked, and trampled upon me with their heavy nailed boots until I was stunned. Then they tied my wrists tightly behind my back; they bound my elbows, my chest, my neck, and my ankles. I was a prisoner!

They lifted me and made me stand up. Brave Chanden Sing had been struggling with all his might against fifteen or twenty foes, and had disabled several of them. He had been pounced upon at the same moment that I was, and had fought gallantly until, like myself, he had been entangled, thrown down, and secured with ropes. During my struggle I heard him call out repeatedly: "*Banduk, banduk, Mansing; jaldi, banduk!*" (Rifle, rifle, Mansing; quick, my rifle!) but, alas, poor Mansing the leper, the weak and jaded coolie, had been sprung upon by four powerful Tibetans, who held him pinned to the ground as if he had been the fiercest of bandits. Mansing was a philosopher. He had saved himself the trouble of even offering a resistance; but he, too, was ill-treated, beaten, and tightly bound. At the beginning of the fight a shrill whistle had brought up four hundred[1] armed soldiers who had lain in ambush round us, concealed behind the

[1] The Lamas stated afterward that this was the number.

innumerable sand-hills and in the depressions in the ground. They took up a position round us and covered us with their matchlocks.

All was now over, and, bound like a criminal, I looked round to see what had become of my men. When I realized that it took the Tibetans five hundred men,[1] all counted, to arrest a starved Englishman and his two half-dying servants, and that, even then, they dared not do it openly, but had to resort to abject treachery; when I found that these soldiers were picked troops from Lhassa and Sigatz (*Shigatze*), dispatched on purpose to arrest our progress and capture us, I could not repress a smile of contempt for those into whose hands we had at last fallen.

My blood boiled when, upon the order of the Lama, who the previous night had professed to be our friend, several men advanced and searched our pockets. They rifled us of everything we possessed. Then they began overhauling our baggage. The watches and chronometer were looked upon with suspicion, their ticking causing curiosity and even anxiety. They were passed round, and mercilessly thrown about from one person to the other until they stopped ticking. They were then pronounced "dead." The compasses and aneroids, which they could not distinguish from watches, were soon thrown aside, as "they had no life in them." Great caution was displayed in touching our rifles, which were lying on our bedding when the tent had been torn down.

Fears were entertained lest the rifles should go off un-

[1] Counting Lamas, villagers, and soldiers.

I WAS A PRISONER

expectedly. It was only on my assurance (which made our captors ten times more cautious) that they were not loaded, that at last they took them and registered them in the catalogue of our confiscated property. I had upon me a gold ring that my mother had given me when I was a child. I asked permission to retain it. With their superstitious nature they immediately thought that it had occult powers, like the wands one reads of in fairy tales.

A man called Nerba, who later on played an important part in our sufferings, was intrusted with the ring, and was warned never to let me see it again. It was heartbreaking, as we three prisoners sat bound and held down by guards, to see the Lamas and officers handle all our things so roughly that they spoiled nearly all they touched. Particularly disgusting was their avidity when, in searching the pockets of the coat I wore daily, and which I had not put on that morning, they found a quantity of silver coins, some eight hundred rupees in all. Officers, Lamas, and soldiers made a grab for the money, and when order was re-established only a few coins remained where the sum had been laid down. Other moneys which they found in one of my loads met with a similar fate. Among the things arousing the greatest curiosity was an india-rubber pillow fully blown out. The soft, smooth texture of the india-rubber seemed to take their fancy. One after the other they rubbed their cheeks on the cushion, exclaiming at the pleasant sensation it gave them. In playing with the brass screw by which the cushion was inflated, they gave it a turn, and the imprisoned air found its way out with a hissing noise. This created quite a panic among the Tibetans. Their superstitious minds regarded this hissing as an evil omen. Naturally I took advantage of any small incident of this kind to work judiciously on their superstitions and to frighten the natives as much as I could.

The Tibetans, having examined all except my water-tight cases of instruments, photographic plates, and sketches, seemed so upset at one or two things that happened, and at some remarks I made, that they hurriedly sealed up my property, which they had placed in bags and wrapped in blankets. They ordered the things to be placed on yaks and brought into the guard-house of the settlement. This done, they tied the end of the ropes that bound our necks to the pommels of their saddles, and, having loosed our feet, they sprang on their ponies and rode off, with shouts, hisses, and cries of victory, firing their matchlocks in the air, and dragging us prisoners into the settlement.

On reaching the settlement, my last words to my men before we were separated were: "No matter what they do to you, do not let them see that you suffer." They promised to obey me. We were conveyed to different tents.

I was dragged to one of the larger tents, inside and outside of which soldiers were placed on guard. They were at first sulky, and rough in their manner and speech. I always made a point of answering them in a collected and polite fashion. I had on many previous occasions noticed that nothing carries one further in dealings with Asiatics than to keep calm and cool. I felt confident that

DRAGGED INTO THE SETTLEMENT

if we were ever to get out of our present scrape, it would be by maintaining a perfectly impassive demeanor in face of anything that might happen.

The tent being kept closed, I was unable to see what was taking place outside, but I could hear the noise of people rushing here and there. Orders were shouted, and the continuous tinkling of the soldiers' horse-bells as they galloped past the tent made me conclude that the place must be in a state of turmoil. I had been some three hours in the tent when a soldier entered and ordered me out.

"They are going to cut off his head," said he to his comrades. Turning round to me, he made a significant gesture with his hand across his neck.

"*Nikutza*" (All right), said I, dryly.

It must not be forgotten that, when a Tibetan hears words to that effect, he usually goes down on his knees and begs for mercy with tears, and sobs, and prayers in profusion. So it is not surprising that the Tibetans were somewhat astonished at my answer. They seemed puzzled as to what to make of it. I was led out with more reluctance than firmness.

During the time I had been shut up a huge white tent with blue ornaments had been pitched in front of the mud house. Round it were hundreds of soldiers and villagers—a most picturesque sight.

As I was led nearer I perceived that the front of the tent was wide open. Inside stood a great number of red Lamas, with shaven heads, and long woollen tunics. The soldiers stopped me when I was about twenty yards from the tent. Additional ropes were added to those already cutting into my wrists, elbows, and chest, and the others were made tighter. I perceived Chanden Sing led forward. Instead of taking me before the Lamas, they pushed me to the back of the mud house to prevent my seeing the scene that followed. I heard Chanden Sing being interrogated in a loud, angry tone of voice, and accused of having been my guide. Next I heard wild shouts from the crowd, then a dead silence. A few instants later I was horrified. I listened—yes, it was the snapping noise of a lash, followed by hoarse moans from my poor servant, to whom they were evidently applying it.

I counted the strokes, the sickening noise of which is still well impressed on my memory, as they regularly and steadily fell one after the other, to twenty, to thirty, forty, and fifty. Then there was a pause.

A number of soldiers now came for me. I was first led, then pushed violently before the tribunal.

On a high seat in the centre of the tent sat a man wearing ample trousers of gaudy yellow and a short yellow coat with flowing sleeves. On his head he had a huge four-pointed hat, gilt all over, and with three great eyes painted on it. He was young-looking. His head was clean shaven, as he was a Lama of the highest order, a Grand Lama and a *Pombo*, or Governor of the province, with powers equivalent to those of a feudal king. On his right stood a stout, powerful red Lama who held a huge double-handed sword. Behind him, and at the sides, were a number of other Lamas, officers and soldiers. As I stood silent, and held my head high before him, two or three Lamas rushed at me and ordered me to kneel. They tried to compel me to do so by forcing me on my knees, but I succeeded in remaining standing.

The Pombo, who was furious at my declining to kneel before him, addressed me in words that sounded violent; but, as he spoke classical Tibetan, and I only the colloquial language, I could not understand a word he said. I meekly asked him not to use such fine words, as they were unintelligible to me.

The great man was taken aback at this request. With a frown on his face, he pointed to me to look to my left. The soldiers and Lamas drew aside, and I beheld Chanden Sing lying flat on his face, stripped from the waist down, in front of a row of Lamas and military men. Two powerful Lamas, one on each side of him, began again to chastise him with knotted leather thongs weighted with lead, laying on their strokes with vigorous arms from his waist to his feet. He was bleeding all over. Each time that a lash fell on his wounded skin, so great was my sorrow that it gave me a pain more intense than if a dagger were stuck into my chest, but I never betrayed my feelings. I knew Orientals too well to show any pity for the man, as this would only have involved a more severe punishment for him. So I looked on at his torture as one would upon a thing of every-day occurrence. The Lamas near me shook their fists under my nose, and explained that my turn would come next. I smiled and repeated the usual "*Nikutza, nikutza*" (Very good, very good).

The Pombo and his officers were puzzled. I could see it plainly by their faces.

The Pombo, an effeminate, juvenile, handsome person, almost hysterical in manner, seemed a splendid subject for hypnotic experiments. I had a good reason to think this. As we shall see later, he had already often been under mesmeric influence. He remained with his eyes fixed upon mine, as if in a trance, for certainly over two minutes.

There was a wonderful and sudden change in the man. His voice, arrogant and angry a few moments before, was now soft and apparently kindly. The Lamas around him were evidently concerned at seeing their lord and master transformed from a foaming fury into the quietest of lambs. They seized me and brought me out of his sight to the spot where Chanden Sing was being chastised. Here again I could not be compelled to kneel, so at last I was allowed to squat down before the Pombo's officers.

Two Lamas produced my note-books and maps, and proceeded to question me closely, saying that, if I spoke the truth, I should be spared; otherwise I should be flogged and then beheaded.

I answered that I would speak the truth, whether they punished me or not.

Dressed in a gaudy red silk coat, with gold embroidery at the collar, one of the Lamas, a great big brute who had taken part in the flogging of Chanden Sing, told me I must say "that my servant had shown me the road across Tibet, and that he had drawn the maps and sketches." If I stated this, they were willing to release me and have me conveyed back to the frontier, promising to do me no further harm. They would cut my servant's head off, that was all, but no personal injury would be inflicted on me.

I explained clearly to the Lamas that I alone was responsible for the maps and sketches, and for finding my way so far into the Forbidden Land. I repeated several times, slowly and distinctly, that my servant was innocent, and that therefore there was no reason to punish him. He had only obeyed my orders in following me to Tibet, and I alone, not my two servants, was to be punished if anybody was punishable.

The Lamas were angry at this. One of them struck me violently on the head with the butt-end of his riding-crop. I pretended not to notice it, though it made my scalp ache to quite an appreciable extent.

"Then we shall beat you and your man until you say what we want!" the Lama exclaimed, angrily.

"You can beat us if you like," I replied, with assurance, "but if you punish us unjustly it will go against yourselves. You can tear our skin off, you can make us bleed to death, but you cannot make us feel pain."

Ando, the traitor, who spoke Hindustani fluently, acted as interpreter whenever there was a hitch in our conversation. With what I knew of the Tibetan language, and with this man's help, everything was explained as clearly as possible to the Tibetans. Notwithstanding this, they continued to lash mercilessly my poor servant. In his agony he was biting the ground as each blow fell on him tearing away patches of skin and flesh. Chanden Sing behaved heroically. Not a word of complaint nor a prayer for mercy came from his lips. He said that he had spoken the truth, and had nothing more to say. Watched intently by all the Lamas and soldiers, I sat with affected calm before this scene of cruelty, until, angry at my indifference, order was given to the soldiers that I should be dragged away. Again they led me behind the mud house, from where I could distinctly hear the angry cries of the Lamas cross-examining Chanden Sing and those dreadful sounds of the lash still being administered on my poor servant.

It began to rain heavily. This was lucky for us, for in Tibet, as in China, a shower has a great effect upon the people. Even massacres have been known to be postponed until the rain stopped.

Such was the case that day. The moment the first drops fell, the soldiers and Lamas rushed here, there, and everywhere inside the tents. I was hastily dragged to the most distant tent of the settlement, which became packed with the soldiers in whose charge I had been given.

CHANDEN SING BEING FLOGGED

CHAPTER XIX

THREATS OF DEATH

An officer of high rank was sitting cross-legged at the farther end of the tent. He wore a handsome dark-red tunic trimmed with gold and leopard skin, and was shod in tall black-and-red leather boots of Chinese shape. A beautiful sword with a solid silver sheath inlaid with large pieces of coral and malachite was passed through his belt.

This man, apparently between fifty and sixty years of age, had an intelligent, refined, honest, good-natured face. I felt that he would be a friend. Indeed, whereas the soldiers and Lamas treated me with brutality and were indescribably mean, this officer alone showed some civility to me. He made room by his side, and asked me to sit there.

"I am a soldier," said he, in a dignified tone, "not a Lama. I have come from Lhassa with my men to arrest you. You are now our prisoner. You have shown no fear, and I respect you."

So saying, he inclined his head and laid his forehead touching mine, and put out his tongue. Then he made a gesture which meant that, though he wished to say more, he could not, owing to the presence of the soldiers.

Later on we entered into a friendly conversation, in

the course of which he said he was a Rupun (a rank below a general). I tried to explain to him all about English soldiers and weapons. He displayed the keenest interest in all I told him. In return he gave me interesting information about the soldiers of Tibet. Every man in Tibet is considered a soldier in time of war or when required to do duty. For the regular army all lads strong and healthy can enlist from the age of seventeen. Good horsemanship is one of the qualities most appreciated in the Tibetan soldier, and, after that, unbounded obedience. The Rupun swore by Tibetan matchlocks, which he believed to be the most serviceable weapons on earth. According to him, as long as you had powder enough, you could use anything as a projectile. Pebbles, earth, or nails did as good work as any lead bullet.

He told me that large quantities of these weapons were manufactured at Lhassa and Sigatz (*Shigatze*). The majority of Tibetan men outside the towns possessed matchlocks. Gunpowder was made in the country with saltpetre and sulphur.

The Rupun, seeing how quick I was at picking up Tibetan words, took a special delight in teaching me, as one would a child, the names of the several grades in the Tibetan army. The *Tchu-pun* was the lowest grade, and only had ten men under him; then came the *Kiatsamba-pun* or *Kia-pun*, or officer in command of one hundred soldiers; and the *Tung-pun*, or head of one thousand. These officers, however, were seldom allowed the full number of soldiers. Often the "commander of one thousand" had only under him three or four hundred men at the most. Above the *Tung-pun* came the *Rupun*, a kind of adjutant-general; then the *Dah-pun*, or great officer; and highest of all, the *Mag-pun* (or *Mag-bun*, as it is usually pronounced), the general-in-chief.

The acquaintance of one of these generals I had already made at Gyanema. Though my informant said that officers were elected for their bravery in war and for their strength and aptitude in the saddle and with their weapons, I knew well enough that such was not the case. The posts were mainly given to whoever could afford to pay for them, among men of families under special protection of the Lamas. In many cases they were actually sold by auction.

The Rupun had a keen sense of humor. I told him how fast the Tibetan soldiers had run away on previous occasions when I had met them and had my rifle with me. He was quite equal to the situation, and exclaimed: "Yes, I know that they ran, but it was not through fear. It was because they did not wish to hurt you." Upon which I answered that, if that were the case, they need not have run so fast.

The Rupun was amused, and laughed at my sarcasm. He patted me on the back, and said I was right. He professed to be grieved to see me tied up. He had received strict orders not to give me food or unloose my bonds.

The soldiers, who had been harsh and rough, listened open-mouthed to the friendly talk between the Rupun and myself, a practice not common in Tibet between captor and prisoner. Following their chief's example they, too, became quite kind and respectful. They placed a cushion under me and tried to make me a little more comfortable.

Toward the evening the Rupun was summoned before the Pombo. The guard was relieved by a fresh lot of men. This was a change for the worse. The new-comers were extremely rough. They dragged me away from the dignified seat I had occupied in the place of honor in the tent, and knocked me violently down on a heap of dung which was there to be used as fuel.

"That is the place for *Plenkis!*" shouted one of the men, "not in the best part of the tent."

They pounced upon me, and though I made no resistance whatever, they again tied my feet together. An additional rope was fastened round my knees. The ends of these ropes were left long, and each was given in charge of a soldier.

No part of a Tibetan tent was ever clean. The spot where I was to rest for the night was the dirtiest. Bound so tightly that the ropes cut grooves in my flesh, it was out of the question to sleep. Worse than this was the disgusting fact that I soon got covered with vermin, which swarmed in the tent. From this time till the end of my captivity, or twenty-five days later, I suffered unspeakable tortures from this pest. The soldiers, with their swords drawn, were all round me inside the tent. More soldiers were posted outside.

The night was full of strange events. Shouts could be heard at intervals from a distance outside, and were answered by some one of the guard inside the tent. They were to keep the men awake and make sure that I was still there.

In the middle of the night the Rupun returned. I noticed that he seemed much upset. He sat by my side. By the light of the flickering fire and a wick burning in a brass bowl filled with butter, I could see on his face an expression of great anxiety. I felt, by the kind way in which he looked at me, that he had grave news to give me. I was not mistaken. He moved me from the dirty place where I had been thrown down helpless by the soldiers, and laid me in a more comfortable and cleaner part of the tent. Then he ordered a soldier to bring me a blanket. Next, to my astonishment, he became very severe, and said he must examine my bonds. He turned quite angry, scolding the soldiers for leaving me so insecurely tied, and proceeded to make the knots firmer, a thing which I felt was impossible. Though he pretended to use all his strength in doing this, I found, much to my amazement, that my bonds were really becoming loosened. He then quickly covered me up with the heavy blanket.

The soldiers were at the other end of the large tent arguing loudly over some paltry matter. The Rupun, stooping low, and making pretence to tuck in the blanket, whispered:

"Your head is to be cut off to-morrow. Escape to-night. There are no soldiers outside."

The good man was actually preparing everything for my flight. He put out the light, and came to sleep by my side. It would have been comparatively easy, when all the men had fallen asleep, to slip from under the tent and steal away. I had got my hands easily out of the ropes, and should have had no difficulty in undoing all my other bonds; but the thought that I should be leaving my two men at the mercy of the Tibetans prevented my carrying the escape into effect. The Rupun, having risen to see that the guard were asleep, lay down again close to me and murmured:

"*Nelon, nelon; paladò*" (They are asleep; go).

Well meant and tempting as the offer was, I told him I must stay with my men.

Having my hands free, I managed to sleep a little during the night. When morning came I slipped my hands again inside the ropes, as I feared they might accuse the Rupun of unloosing my hands, and he might be punished on my account.

The Rupun, who seemed much disappointed, tied the ropes round my wrists firmly again. Though he appeared vexed at my not availing myself of the chance of flight he had given me, he treated me with ever-increasing respect and deference. He even produced his wooden bowl, which he filled with steaming tea from the *raksang*, and lifted it up to my mouth for me to drink.

On perceiving how thirsty and hungry I was, not only did this good man refill the cup time after time until my thirst was quenched, but he mixed with it *tsamba* and lumps of butter, which he then stuffed into my mouth with his fingers.

It was really touching to see how, moved to kindness, the soldiers imitated his example, and, one after the other, produced handfuls of *tsamba* and *chura*, and deposited them in my mouth. Their hands were not overclean, but on such occasions it does not do to be too particular. I was so hungry that the food they gave me seemed delicious. I had been for two nights and one day without food, and, what with the exertion of the fight and my various exciting experiences during that time, my appetite was very keen.

The great politeness and consideration with which not only the Rupun, but even the soldiers, now treated me made me suspect that my end was near. I was grieved not to be able to obtain news of Chanden Sing and Mansing. The soldiers' reticence in answering questions regarding them made me fear that something terrible had happened. Nevertheless, though my jailers were friendly, I did not betray anxiety, but pretended to take all that came as a matter of course. I spent the first portion of the day in a lively conversation with the soldiers, partly to divert my thoughts and partly to improve my knowledge of Tibetan.

CHAPTER XX

A TERRIBLE RIDE

EARLY in the afternoon a soldier entered the tent, and striking me on the shoulder with his heavy hand, shouted: "*Ohe!*" (This is a Tibetan exclamation always used by the rougher classes when beginning a conversation. It corresponds to "Look here.")

"*Ohe!*" repeated he; "before the sun goes down you will be flogged, both your legs will be broken,[1] they will burn out your eyes, and then they will cut off your head!"

The man, who seemed quite in earnest, accompanied each sentence with an appropriate gesture to illustrate his words. I laughed at him and affected to treat the whole thing as a joke, partly because I thought this was the best way to frighten them, and partly because the programme thus laid before me seemed so extensive that I thought it could only be intended to intimidate me.

The words of the soldier cast a gloom over my friendly guard in the tent. When I tried to cheer them up, they answered bluntly that I would not laugh for very long. Something was certainly happening. The men rushed in and out of the tent and whispered among themselves.

[1] A form of torture which consists in placing the legs upon two parallel logs of wood. They are then fractured by a heavy blow struck with a mallet.

When I spoke to them they would answer no more, and on my insisting to receive an answer they made signs that their lips must from now be closed.

About half an hour later another person, in a great state of excitement, rushed into the tent and signalled to my guards to lead me out. This they did, after making my bonds tighter than ever, and placing extra ropes round my chest and arms. In this fashion I was marched off to the mud house and led into one of the rooms. A large number of soldiers and villagers assembled outside. After we had waited some time, Mansing, tightly bound, was brought into the same room. My pleasure at seeing my man again was so great that I paid no attention to the insults of the mob peeping through the door. After a while a Lama came in with a smiling face, and said he had good news to give me.

"We have ponies here," he said, "and we are going to take you back to the frontier, but the Pombo wishes to see you first to-day. Do not make a resistance. Let us exchange the ropes round your wrists for these iron handcuffs."

Here he produced a heavy pair of manacles which he had kept concealed under his coat.

"You will not wear them for more than a few moments, while we are leading you to his presence. Then you will be free. We swear to you by the Sun and Kunjuk-Sum that we will treat you kindly."

I promised not to resist, chiefly because I had no chance of doing so. For greater safety they tied my legs and placed a sliding knot round my neck; then I was carried out into the open, where a ring of soldiers with drawn swords stood round me. They made me lay flat on my face on the ground, and held me down firmly while they unwound the ropes from around my wrists. The iron fetters, joined by a heavy chain, were substituted for them. They took some time in fastening the clumsy padlock, after which, all being ready, they unbound my legs.

When I stood up again, and knowing that I could not possibly get my hands free, they began to load me with insults, not directed to me as an individual, but as a *Plenki* (an Englishman). They spat upon me and threw mud at me. The Lamas behaved worse than any of the others. The one who had sworn that I should in no way be ill-used if I submitted quietly to be handcuffed was the most prominent among my tormentors and the keenest in urging the crowd on to further brutality.

Suddenly the attention of the crowd was drawn to the approach of the Rupun with a number of soldiers and officers. He seemed depressed. His face was of a ghastly yellowish tint. He kept his eyes fixed on the ground. Speaking in a low tone of voice, he ordered that I should again be conveyed inside the mud house.

A few moments later he came in and closed the door after him, having first cleared the room of all the people who were in it. Tibetan structures of this kind have a square aperture in the ceiling by which they are ventilated and lighted.

The Rupun laid his forehead upon mine in sign of compassion, and then sadly shook his head.

"There is no more hope," he whispered; "your head will be cut off to-night. The Lamas are bad. My heart is aching. You are like my brother, and I am grieved...."

The good old man tried not to let me see his emotion, and made signs that he could stay no longer, lest he should be accused of being my friend.

The mob again entered the room. I was once more dragged out into the open by the Lamas and soldiers. Some discussion followed as to who should keep the key of my handcuffs, and eventually it was handed over to one of the officers, who mounted his pony and rode away at a great speed in the direction of Lhassa.

Just then I heard the voice of Chanden Sing calling to me in a weak, agonized tone:

"*Hazur, hazur, hum murgiaega!*" (Sir, sir, I am dying!) Turning my head in the direction from which these painful sounds came, I perceived my faithful servant with his hands bound behind his back, dragging himself on his stomach toward the door of one of the other rooms of the mud house. His poor face was hardly recognizable, it bore the traces of such awful suffering.

I could stand no more. Pushing my guards aside with my shoulders, I endeavored to get to the poor wretch, and had nearly reached him when soldiers sprang upon me, grappled me, and lifting me bodily off my feet, threw me on the back of a pony.

I now feared the worst. I tried to encourage my brave servant by shouting to him that I was being taken to Taklakot, and that he would be brought after me the following day. He had exhausted his last atom of strength in creeping to the door. He was roughly seized, and brutally hurled back into the room of the mud house, so that we could not exchange a word more. Mansing, the coolie, was placed, with his arms pinioned, on a bare-back pony.

The saddle of the pony I had been thrown upon is worthy of description. It was in reality the wooden frame of a very high-backed saddle, like a Mexican saddle. From the highest point of the back five or six sharp iron spikes stuck out horizontally. As I sat on this implement of torture, I was not actually sitting on the spikes, but the spikes caught me in the back just below the waist.

My guard having been augmented by twenty or thirty mounted men with muskets and swords, we set off at a furious pace. A horseman riding in front of me led my pony by means of a cord, as my hands were manacled behind my back. Thus we travelled across country for many miles.

Except for those awful spikes in the saddle, the ride would not have been so bad. The pony I rode was a spirited animal, and the country around was curious and interesting. We proceeded along a succession of yellow sand-hills, some of them as high as two or three hundred feet, others not more than twenty or thirty feet. The sand seemed to have been deposited more by wind than water, though it is also possible that the whole basin, not very high above the level of the huge stream, may at some time have been altogether under water. The whole space between the mountain range to the north of the Brahmaputra and the river itself was covered with these sand-mounds, except in certain places where the soil was extremely marshy. Here our ponies sank in deep, soft mud. We splashed across several rivulets and skirted a number of ponds. From the summit of a hill on which they led me, I could see that the hills were of much greater circumference and height near the river, becoming smaller and smaller as they approached the mountain range to the north. They increased in number and size the farther we went in an easterly direction.

The circumstances under which I was now travelling did not permit me to make accurate investigations as to where the sand came from. A mere glance at the country all round made me feel sure that the sand had been conveyed from the south. This could be plainly seen from depressions and wave-like undulations, showing that it had travelled (roughly) in a northerly direction. I was fairly convinced that the sand had been deposited there by the wind, which had carried it from the plains of India over the Himahlyan chain.

My guard scoured the country from the high point of vantage on which we had ascended. Away in the distance, to the east, we saw a large number of horsemen raising clouds of dust. Riding down the hill, our ponies sinking in soft sand, we set off in the direction of the newcomers, the ground at the bottom of the hill being somewhat harder.

We travelled mile after mile at an unpleasant pace, until we arrived at a spot where, drawn up in a line, was the cavalcade we had seen from the summit of the hill. It was a beautiful sight as we approached it, though the pain which I was undergoing rather detracted from the pleasure I should otherwise have taken in the picturesque scene. There were about a hundred red Lamas in the centre, with bannermen whose heads were covered by peculiar flat fluffy hats, and an equal number of soldiers and officers in their gray, red, and black tunics—some two hundred horsemen in all.

The Pombo, in his yellow coat and trousers and his queer pointed hat, sat on a magnificent pony in front of the crowd of Lamas and soldiers.

Curiously enough, when close to this new crowd, the horseman who led my pony let go the rope, and the pony was lashed cruelly and left to run wildly. The soldiers of my guard reined up and drew aside. The pony dashed off in the direction of the Pombo, and, as I passed close to him, a man whose name I learned afterward was Nerba (a private secretary of the Tokchim Tarjum) knelt down, and, taking aim with his matchlock resting on its prop, deliberately fired a shot at me.

Although Nerba was considered one of the champion shots of the country, and the distance from the muzzle of his matchlock to me was not more than four yards, the bullet missed me, whizzing past my left ear. Probably the speed at which my animal was proceeding saved me, as the marksman could not take a steady aim. My pony, startled at the sudden report of the matchlock at such close quarters, took fright, and began rearing and plunging. I managed to maintain my seat, though the spikes in the saddle were lacerating terribly the lower part of my spine.

Several horsemen now rode up and captured my pony. Preparations were made for another exciting number in the programme of my tortures. In a way these Lamas possessed a sporting nature, but I swore to myself that, no matter what they did to me, I would not give them the satisfaction of seeing that they were hurting me. Acting on this principle, I pretended not to feel the effect of the spikes tearing the flesh off my backbone. When they led me before the Pombo to show him how covered with blood I was, I expressed satisfaction at riding such an excellent pony. This seemed to puzzle him.

A cord of yak-hair, about forty or fifty yards long, was now produced. The swivel attached to one end was fastened to my handcuffs, and the other end was held by a horseman. We set off again on our wild career, this time followed not only by the guard, but by the Pombo and all his men. Once or twice I could not help turning round to look at them. The cavalcade was a weird and picturesque sight, the riders with their many-colored dresses, their matchlocks with red flags, their jewelled swords, their banners with long ribbons of all colors flying in the wind—all galloping furiously, shouting, yelling, and hissing, amid a deafening din of thousands of horse-bells.

In order to quicken our speed, a horseman rode by my side lashing my pony to make it go its hardest. Meanwhile the horseman who held the cord did his utmost to pull me off the saddle, no doubt in the hope of seeing me trampled to death by the cavalcade behind me. As I leaned my body forward so as to maintain my seat, and with my arms pulled violently backward by the rope, the flesh on my hands and knuckles was rubbed off down to the bone by the chain of the handcuffs. Every tug brought me into forcible contact with the spikes and inflicted deep wounds. The cord eventually and unexpectedly gave way. The soldier who was pulling at the other end was clumsily unhorsed, and I myself was all but thrown by the unexpected jerk. This amusing incident at first provoked mirth among my escort, a mirth which their superstitious minds immediately turned into an ill omen.

When my pony was stopped, as well as the runaway steed of the dismounted cavalier, I took advantage of their fears, and assured them once more that whatever harm they tried to do me would go against themselves. However, the cord was retied with sundry strong knots, and, after an interruption of a few minutes, we resumed our breakneck gallop, I being again sent in front.

Toward the end of our journey we had to go round the curve of a sand-hill, the track between this and a large pond at its foot being very narrow. At this point I saw in front of me a soldier posted in ambush, with his matchlock ready to fire. The pony sank deep in the sand, and could not travel fast, which, I suppose, was the reason why that spot had been selected. The man fired as I passed only a few paces from him; but, as luck would have it, this second attempt also left me untouched.

Getting clear of the soft sand, and finding harder ground, we resumed our headlong career. Several arrows were shot at me from behind. Some passed very near, but not one struck me. Thus, after an interminable ride

THE RIDE ON A SPIKED SADDLE

full of incident and excitement, near sunset we arrived at our destination.

On the crown of a hill stood a fortress and large Lamasery. At its foot, in front of a large structure, the Pombo's gaudy tent had been pitched. The name of this place, as far as I could afterward ascertain, was Namj Laccé Galshio or Gyatsho.

CHAPTER XXI

THE EXECUTIONER

Two or three men tore me roughly off the saddle. The pain in my spine caused by the spikes was intense. I asked for a moment's rest. My captors refused to let me stop, and, roughly thrusting me forward, said I would be beheaded in an instant. All the people round jeered and made signs to me that my head would be cut off. Insults of all kinds were showered upon me by the crowd of Lamas and soldiers. I was hustled to the execution-ground, which lay to the left front of the tent. On the ground was a long log of wood in the shape of a prism. Upon the sharp edge of this I was made to stand. Several men held me by the body while four or five others, using their combined strength, stretched my legs wide apart. Fixed in this painful position, the Tibetans securely tied my feet to the log of wood with cords of yak-hair. Several men were made to pull these cords, and they were so tight that they cut into my skin and flesh in several places round my ankles and on my feet. Many of the cuts were as much as three inches long.[1]

When I was thus firmly bound, the man Nerba, whom I have mentioned before as having fired a shot at me, came forward, and then, going behind me, seized me by the hair

[1] Measured some weeks later by Doctor Wilson.

of my head. My hair was long, as it had not been cut for more than five months.

The sight before me was impressive. By the Pombo's tent stood in a row the most villanous brutes I have ever set eyes upon. One, a powerful, repulsive individual, held in his hand a great knobbed mallet used for fracturing bones; another carried a bow and arrows; a third held a big two-handed sword; others made a display of various ghastly instruments of torture. The crowd, thirsting for my blood, formed up in a semicircle, leaving room for me to see the parade of the torture implements that awaited me. As my eyes roamed from one figure to the other, the several Lamas shook their various implements to show that they were preparing for action.

A group of three Lamas stood at the entrance of the tent. They were the musicians. One held a gigantic horn, which, when blown, emitted hoarse, thundering sounds. His companions had one a drum, the other cymbals. Another fellow some distance away continually sounded a huge gong. From the moment I was made to dismount the deafening sounds of the diabolical music echoed all through the valley, and added horror to the scene.

An iron bar with a handle of wood bound in red cloth was being made red-hot in a brazier. The Pombo, who had placed something in his mouth in order to produce artificial foaming at the lips, and thus show his fury, worked himself into a frenzy. A Lama handed him the implement of torture (the *taram*), now red-hot. The Pombo seized it by the handle.

"*Ngaghi kiu meh taxon!*" (We will burn out your eyes!) cried a chorus of Lamas.

The Pombo strode up to me, brandishing the ghastly implement. He seemed reluctant, but the Lamas around him urged him on, lifting the man's arm toward me.

"You have come to this country to see" (alluding to what I had stated the previous day—*viz.*, that I was a traveller and pilgrim, and had only come to see the country). "This, then, is the punishment for you!" and with these dreadful words the Pombo raised his arm and placed the red-hot iron bar parallel to, and about an inch or two from, my eyeballs, and all but touching my nose.

Instinctively I kept my eyes closed, but the heat was so intense that it seemed as if my eyes, the left one especially, were being desiccated and my nose scorched.

Though the time seemed interminable, I do not think that the heated bar was before my eyes actually longer than thirty seconds or so. Yet it was quite long enough, for, when I lifted my aching eyelids, I saw everything as in a red mist. My left eye was frightfully painful, and every few seconds it seemed as if something in front of it obscured its vision. With the right eye I could still see fairly well, except that everything, as I have said, looked red instead of its usual color. The hot iron was then thrown down, and was frizzling on the wet ground a few paces from me.

My position was not enviable, as I stood with my legs wide apart, with my back, hands, and legs bleeding, and my sight injured. This amid the deafening, maddening noise of the gong, drum, cymbals, and horn; insulted, spat upon by the crowd, and with Nerba holding me so tight by my hair that he tore handfuls of it from my scalp. All I could do was to remain calm and composed, and to await with apparent unconcern the preparations for the next sufferings to be inflicted upon me.

"*Miumta nani sehko!*" (Kill him with a rifle!) shouted a hoarse voice.

A matchlock was now being loaded by a soldier, and such was the quantity of gunpowder they placed in the barrel that I made sure whoever fired it would have his head blown off. It was with a certain amount of satisfaction that I saw it handed over to the Pombo. That official placed the side of the weapon against my forehead with the muzzle pointing skyward. Then a soldier, leaning down, applied fire to the fusee. Eventually there was a loud report, which gave my head a severe shock. The overloaded matchlock flew clean out of the Pombo's hand, much to everybody's surprise. I forced myself to laugh. The tantalizing failure of every attempt they made to hurt me drove the crowd to the highest pitch of fury.

"*Ta kossaton, ta kossaton!*" (Kill him, kill him!) exclaimed fierce voices all around me. "*Ngala mangbo shidak majidan!*" (We cannot frighten him!) "*Ta kossaton, ta kossaton!*" (Kill him, kill him!) The whole valley resounded with these ferocious cries.

A huge two-handed sword was now handed to the Pombo, who drew it out of its sheath.

"Kill him, kill him!" shouted the mob once more,

urging on the executioner, who seemed quite reluctant to come forward.

I seized this moment to say that they might kill me if they wished, but that, if I died to-day, they would all die to-morrow—an undeniable fact, for we are all bound to die some day. This seemed to cool them for a moment; but the excitement in the crowd was too great, and at last they succeeded in working the Pombo into a passion. His face became quite unrecognizable, such was his excitement. He behaved like a madman.

At this point a Lama approached and slipped something into the mouth of the executioner, who foamed at the lips. A Lama held his sword, while he turned up one sleeve of his coat to have his arm free, and the Lamas turned up the other for him. Then he strode toward me with slow, ponderous steps, swinging the shiny, sharp blade from side to side, with his bare arms outstretched.

The man Nerba, who was still holding me by the hair, was told to make me bend my neck. I resisted with what little strength I had left, determined to keep my head erect and my forehead high. They might kill me, true enough, they might hack me to pieces if they chose, but never until I had lost my last atom of strength would these ruffians make me stoop before them. I might perish, but it would be looking down upon the Pombo and his countrymen.

The executioner, now close to me, held the sword with his nervous hands, lifting it high above his shoulder. He then brought it down to my neck, which he touched with the blade, to measure the distance as it were, for a clean, effective stroke. Then, drawing back a step, he quickly raised the sword again and struck a blow at me with all his might. The sword passed unpleasantly close to my neck under my chin, but did not touch me. I did not flinch nor speak. My indifference impressed him almost to the point of frightening him. He seemed disinclined to continue his diabolical performance; but the impatience and turbulence of the crowd were at their highest. The Lamas nearer him gesticulated like madmen and urged him on again.

Apparently against his will, the executioner went through the same performance on the other side of my head. This time the blade passed so near that the point cannot have been more than half an inch or so from my neck.

Everything pointed toward my end being near; but, strange to say, I had a feeling all the time that something would happen and my life would be spared. As the chances of escape, however, seemed very meagre, I felt sorry that I should have to die without seeing my dear parents and relatives again. They would probably never know where and how I had died. After my trying experiences, sufferings, and excitement since entering Tibet, I did not, perhaps, realize my peril so much as I should have done had I, for instance, been dragged from my comfortable London quarters direct on to the execution-ground.

Naturally the scene was one that I am not likely to forget, and I must say for the Tibetans that the whole affair was picturesquely carried out. Even the ghastliest ceremonies may have their artistic side, and this particular one, performed with extra pomp and flourish, was really impressive.

It appears that the unpleasant sword exercise is sometimes gone through in Tibet previous to actually cutting off the head, so as to make the victim suffer mentally as much as possible before the final blow is given. It is also done in order to display the wonderful skill of the executioner in handling the big sword. I was not aware of this at the time, and only learned it some weeks after. It is usually at the third stroke that the victim is actually beheaded.

The Lamas were still clamoring for my head, but the Pombo made a firm stand this time, and declined to go on with the execution. They collected round him and seemed very angry. They shouted and yelled and gesticulated in the wildest fashion, and still the Pombo kept his eyes fixed upon me in a half-respectful, half-frightened manner, and refused to move.

An excited consultation followed, during which, in the midst of this scene of barbarity, my coolie Mansing arrived. He had fallen off his bare-back pony many times, and had been left far behind. The man who held my hair now relinquished his grasp, while another pushed me violently from in front, causing me to fall heavily backward, and putting a painful strain on all the tendons of my legs. Mansing, bruised and aching all over, was brought forward and tied by his legs to the same log of wood to which I was fastened. They informed me that they would kill my coolie first. One brutal Lama seized him roughly by the throat. I was pushed up in a sitting posture. A cloth was thrown over my head and face, so that I could not see what they were doing. I heard poor Mansing groan pitifully, then there was a dead silence. I called him, but received no answer, so I concluded that he had been killed. I was left in this terrible suspense for over a quarter of an hour, when at last they removed the cloth from over my head, and I saw my coolie lying before me, bound to the log and almost unconscious, but, thank God, still alive. He told me that, when I had called him, a Lama had placed his hand upon his mouth to prevent him from answering, while, with the other hand, the Lama had squeezed his neck so tightly as to nearly strangle him. Mansing's coolness and bravery during these terrible trials were really marvellous.

We were told that our execution was only postponed till the next day, in order that we might be tortured until the time came for us to be put to death.

A number of Lamas and soldiers stood round jeering at us. I seized this opportunity to hail a swaggering Lama and ask him for some refreshment.

"*Orcheh, orcheh nga dappa tugu duh, chuen deh, dang, yak, guram, tcha, tsamba pin!*" (I am very hungry; please give me some rice, yak meat, *ghur*, tea, and oatmeal!) I asked, in my best Tibetan.

"*Hum murr, Maharaja!*" (I want butter, your Majesty!) put in Mansing, half in Hindustani and half in the Tibetan language.

This natural application for food seemed to afford intense amusement to our torturers. They formed a ring round us, and laughed at our appeal, while Mansing and I, both of us famished, were left bound in a most painful position.

The day had now waned. Our torturers did not fail to constantly remind us that the following day our heads would be severed from our bodies. I told them that it would cause us no pain, for if they gave us no food we should probably be dead from starvation by then.

Whether they realized that this might be the case, or whether some other reason moved them, I cannot say. Several Lamas, who had been most brutal, including one who had the previous day taken part in Chanden Sing's flogging, now became quite polite and treated us with a surprising amount of deference. Two Lamas were dispatched to the monastery, and returned after some time with bags of *tsamba* and a large *raksang* of boiling tea. I have hardly ever enjoyed a meal more, though the Lamas stuffed the food down my throat with their unwashed fingers so fast that they nearly choked me.

"Eat, eat as much as you can," said they, grimly, "for it may be your last meal."

And eat I did, and washed the *tsamba* down with quantities of buttered tea, which they poured into my mouth carelessly out of the *raksang*.

Mansing, whose religion did not allow him to eat food touched by people of a different caste, was eventually permitted to lick the meal out of the wooden bowl. I myself was none too proud to take the food in any way it might be offered, and when my humble "*Orcheh, orcheh tchuen mangbo terokchi!*" (Please give me some more!) met with the disapproval of the Lamas, and brought out the everlasting negative, "*Middù, middù,*" I was still too hungry to waste any of the precious food given us. Upon application the Tibetans revolved the wooden bowl round and round my mouth, and I licked it as clean as if it had never been used.

After all the excitement of the day, we were beginning to feel a little better. It was a great relief to be treated less roughly, were it only for a few moments, when, small as it was, the improvement in our condition was checked.

A Lama came from the monastery and gave orders right and left. The place was again in commotion. We were pounced upon and roughly seized. My legs were quickly untied, a number of men holding me down the while. Again they lifted me until I stood upright on the cutting edge of the prismatic log; two men seized one leg and two the other, and stretched them apart as far as they could possibly go. Then rope after rope was wound round my feet and ankles, and I was made fast as before to the log.

As my legs were much farther apart this time, the pain in the muscles of my legs when they proceeded to knock me down backward was even greater than it had been on the previous occasion. But before I had time to feel it in full, the Lamas, now as ferocious as they were at first, dragged my manacled arms backward from under my body and tied a rope to the chain of the handcuffs. This done, they passed the rope through a hole in the top of a high post behind me, and by tugging at it, strained my arms upward in a way that, had I been less supple, would certainly have broken them. When all their strength combined could not stretch me another inch without tearing my body to pieces, they made the rope fast, and I remained half suspended, and feeling as if all the bones of my limbs were getting pulled out of their sockets. The weight of the body naturally tending to settle down would, I felt, every moment increase the suffering of this terrible torture, which was really a primitive form of the rack.

Mansing was likewise suspended opposite me. His feet were tied to the log to which my own were fastened, only not quite so wide apart.

The pain was at first intense, the tendons of the legs and arms being dreadfully strained, and the spinal column bent so as to be nearly broken in two. The shoulder-blades, forced into close contact, pressed the vertebræ inward, and caused excruciating pains along the lumbar vertebræ, where the strain was greatest.

As if this were not sufficient, a cord was tied from Mansing's neck to mine, the object of which was to keep our necks stretched in a most uncomfortable position.

It began to rain heavily. We were left out in the open. The rags to which our clothes had been reduced in our struggle when we were first seized were drenched. Half naked and wounded, we were alternately numbed with cold and burning with fever. A guard encircled us, having with them two watch-dogs tied to pegs. The soldiers were apparently so confident of our inability to escape that they drew their heavy blankets over their heads and slept. One of them in his slumber moved and pushed his sword outside the blanket in which he had rolled himself tight. This inspired me with the idea of attempting to escape.

Two or three hours later the night was dark. Thanks to the exceptionally supple nature of my hands, I succeeded in drawing the right hand out of my handcuffs, and, after an hour or so of stealthy and anxious work, I managed to unloose the cord that bound Mansing's feet. I whispered to him to get up slowly and to push the sword toward me with his foot until I could reach it. If successful in this, I could soon cut my bonds and those fastening Mansing's hands, and with a weapon in our possession we would make a bold dash for liberty.

Mansing, however, was not a champion of agility. In his joy at feeling partly free, the poor coolie moved his stiff legs clumsily. The vigilant watch-dogs detected this, and gave the alarm by barking. The guards were up in a moment. Timid as they always were, they all hurriedly left us, and went to fetch lights in order to examine our bonds.

In the meanwhile, protected by the darkness of the stormy night, I had succeeded in replacing my hand inside the iron handcuff. Putting it back was more difficult than drawing it out, but I just managed to do it in time. The men who had gone to the monastery returned with lights. I pretended to be fast asleep: a likely thing with every bone in my body feeling as if it were disjointed, every limb half numbed and frozen, every tendon so strained as to drive me mad with pain!

The Tibetans found the bonds round Mansing's feet undone. They examined my hands and saw them just as they had left them. They inspected my feet. The ropes were still there cutting into my flesh. They inspected Mansing's hands, only to find them still fastened to the post behind.

The Tibetans were so puzzled at this mysterious occurrence that they positively got frightened. They began to shout excitedly, calling for help. In a moment the alarm was given, a crowd of men rushed at us, and, with their swords drawn, surrounded us. One man, braver than the rest, gave Mansing a few cuts with a whip, warning us that if the ropes were found undone again they would decapitate us there and then. The coolie was again bound more tightly than ever.

CHAPTER XXII

A CHARMED LIFE

By way of precaution, a light was set between Mansing and myself, and, as it was still raining hard, the Tibetans placed a canvas shelter over us to prevent the light from being extinguished. At about six or seven in the morning Mansing's feet were untied, but not his hands. I was left in the same uncomfortable and painful posture. The hours passed slowly and wearily. My legs, my arms, and hands had gradually become quite lifeless. After the first six or seven hours that I had been stretched on the rack, I felt no more actual pain. The numbness crept along every limb of my body, until I had now the peculiar sensation of possessing a living head on a dead body.

The day now dawning was one full of strange incidents. When the sun was high in the sky, the Pombo, with a great number of Lamas, rode down from the monastery, a short distance away. He went to his tent. Soon after, my cases of scientific instruments were brought outside and opened, the soldiers and Lamas displaying an amusing mixture of curiosity and caution over everything they touched. I had to explain the use of each instrument, a difficult matter indeed, considering their ignorance and my limited knowledge of Tibetan, which did not allow of my delivering scientific lectures in their language.

The sextant was looked upon with great suspicion, and even more so the hypsometrical apparatus, with its thermometers in brass tubes, which they took to be some sort of firearm. Then came a lot of undeveloped photographic plates, box after box of which they opened in broad daylight, destroying in a few moments all the valuable negatives that I had taken since leaving Mansarowar. The Pombo, more observant than the others, noticed that the plates turned into a yellowish color on being exposed to the light.

"Why is that?" he asked.

"It is a sign that you will suffer for what you are doing to me."

The Pombo flung away the plate he had picked up and was much upset. He ordered a hole to be dug in the ground some way off, and all the plates to be instantly buried. The soldiers, however, who had been intrusted with the order, seemed loath to touch the plates, and they had to be reprimanded and beaten by the Lamas, before they would obey. At last, with their feet, they pushed the boxes of negatives to a spot some distance off, where, in dog fashion, they dug a deep hole with their hands in the muddy ground. There my precious photographic work of several weeks was covered with earth forever.

Now came my paint-box with its cakes of watercolors.

. "What do you do with these?" cried an angry Lama, pointing at the harmless colors.

"I paint pictures."

"No, you are lying. With the 'yellow' you find where

gold is in the country, and with the 'blue' you discover where malachite is."

I assured them that this was not the case, and told them that if they would untie me I would, on recovering the use of my arms, paint a picture before them.

They prudently preferred to leave me tied up.

Their whole attention was now drawn to a considerable sum in silver and gold which they found in the pack-cases. The Pombo warned the people that not one coin must be stolen.

I took this chance to make an offering of five hundred rupees to the Lamasery. I also told the Pombo that I should like him to accept as a gift my Martini-Henry rifle, which I noticed rather took his fancy.

Both gifts were refused. They said the Lamasery was very rich, and the Pombo's position as an official did not allow him to carry a rifle. The Pombo, nevertheless, fully appreciated the offer, and came personally to thank me.

In a way the rascals were gentlemanly enough in their manner. I could not help admiring their mixture of courtesy and cruelty, either of which they could switch on at a moment's notice regardless of the other.

They had now reached the bottom of a water-tight case. The Pombo drew out with much suspicion a curious flattened article.

"What is that?" inquired he, lifting the thing up in the air.

My sight had been so injured that at that distance I could not clearly discern what it was; but when they waved it in front of my nose, I recognized it to be my long-mislaid bath-sponge, dry and flattened, which Chanden Sing, with his usual ability for packing, had stored away at the bottom of the box, piling upon it the heavy cases of photographic plates. The sponge, a large one, was now reduced to the thickness of less than an inch, owing to the weight that had for weeks lain upon it.

The Tibetans were greatly puzzled at this new discovery. They had never seen or even heard of sponges. Some said it resembled tinder. The wiser Lamas said it might explode. It was touched with caution.

When their curiosity was satisfied, they threw it away. It fell near me in a small pool of water. This was a golden opportunity to frighten my jailers. I addressed the sponge in English, and with any word that came in my head, pretending to utter incantations. The attention of the Lamas and soldiers was quickly drawn to this unusual behavior on my part. They could not conceal their terror when, as I spoke louder and louder to the sponge, it gradually swelled to its normal size with the moisture it absorbed.

The Tibetans, who at first could hardly believe their eyes at this incomprehensible occurrence, became panic-stricken at what they believed to be an exhibition of my occult powers. There was a general stampede in every direction.

In a way, all this was entertaining. Anyhow, it served to pass away the time. The most amusing scene that afternoon was, however, still to come.

After some time the Lamas screwed up their courage,

and returned to where my baggage had been overhauled. One of them picked up my Martini-Henry. The others urged him to fire it off. He came to me, and when I had explained to him how to load it, he took a cartridge and placed it in the breech, but would insist on not closing the bolt firmly home. When I warned him of the consequences, he struck me on the head with the butt of the rifle.

It is the fashion, when aiming with one of their matchlocks, which have a prop attached to them, to place the butt in front of the nose instead of holding it firmly against the shoulder, as we do. So the Lama aimed in this fashion at one of my yaks peacefully grazing some thirty yards off. While everybody watched attentively to see the result of this marksman's shooting, he pulled the trigger; the rifle went off with an extra loud report, and behold! the rifle burst and the violent recoil gave the Lama a fearful blow in the face. The rifle, flying out of his hands, described a somersault in the air, and the Lama fell backward to the ground, where he remained spread out flat, bleeding all over, and screaming like a child. His nose was squashed, one eye had been put out, and his teeth were shattered.

Whether the rifle burst because the bolt had not been properly closed, or because mud had got into the muzzle, I could not say.

The injured Lama was the one at the head of the party that wanted to have my head cut off, so, naturally enough, I could not help betraying my satisfaction at the accident. I was glad they had let me live another day, were it only to see this amusing scene.

The Pombo, who had been, during the greater part of the afternoon, looking at me with an air of mingled pity and respect, as though he had been forced against his will to treat me so brutally, could not help joining in my laughter at the Lama's sorrowful plight. In a way, I believe he was rather glad the accident had happened; for, if he had until then been uncertain whether to kill me or not, he felt, after what had occurred, that it was not prudent to attempt it.

The gold ring which had been seized from me on the day of our arrest, and for which I asked many times, as it had been given me by my mother, was regarded as possessing miraculous powers as long as it was upon or near me. It was therefore kept away from me, for fear that, with its help, I might break my bonds and escape.

The Pombo, the Lamas, and officers held another consultation, at the end of which, toward sunset, several soldiers came and loosed my legs from the stretching log. My hands, though still manacled, were lowered from the pillar behind.

As the ropes round my ankles were unwound from the deep channels they had cut into my flesh, large patches of skin came away with them. Thus ended the most terrible twenty-four hours[1] I have ever passed in my lifetime.

I felt very little relief at first as I lay flat on the ground. My body and legs were stiff as if dead. As time went by and I saw no signs of their coming back to life, I feared that mortification had set in, and that I had lost the use of my feet forever. It was two or three hours before

[1] From sunset one evening to sunset next day.

the blood began to circulate in my right foot. The pain when it did so was intense. Had a handful of knives been passed slowly down the inside of my leg the agony could not have been more excruciating. My arms were not quite so bad. They also were numbed, but the circulation was more quickly re-established.

The Pombo, whether to amuse me or to show off his riches, ordered to be displayed before me about one hundred ponies, some with magnificent harness. Mounting the finest pony and holding in his hand the dreadful *taram*, he rode round the hill on which the monastery and fort stood.

On returning he harangued his men. A series of sports followed, the Pombo seating himself near me and watching me intently to see how I was enjoying the performance. First of all the best marksmen were selected. With their matchlocks they fired one after the other at my two yaks, only a few yards off. Although they aimed carefully, no one succeeded in hitting them. I knew they fired with bullets, for I could hear the hissing sound of the missiles.

Next came an interesting display of horsemanship. I should have enjoyed it more had I not been suffering agonies all the time. The performance helped to cheer me. First there were races in which only two ponies at a time took part, the last race being run between two winners. A *kata* was presented to the final winner. Next one horseman rode ahead full gallop flying a *kata*, while some others followed closely behind. The *kata* was dropped. When it settled on the ground, the horsemen following the leader rode away, and, at a given signal, galloped back wildly, converging toward the *kata*, attempting to pick it up without dismounting. Some of the younger men were very clever at this game.

Another sport consisted in one man on foot being seized and lifted on to the saddle by a mounted comrade riding full gallop.

Though I could not see as well as I wished, I enjoyed the show, and expressed admiration for the ponies. The Pombo thoughtfully ordered the best of them to be brought closer to me, and had me lifted into a sitting posture, so that I could see them better.

This was a great relief. I was suffering more from my humiliating position, being unable to stand, than from the tortures themselves, bad as they were. The Pombo told me that I must now look toward the tent. He then got up and walked toward it.

The opening of the tent was over twenty feet long. Some soldiers came and dragged me close in front of it, so that I could witness all that went on.

Two powerful Lamas entered the tent with the Pombo. A number of other people who were inside were turned out. They closed the tent for a few minutes, and then opened it again. In the mean time a gong summoned the Lamas from the monastery and, a few minutes later, a procession of them came down and took their places inside the tent.

The Pombo, in his yellow coat and trousers and four-pointed hat, sat on a high-backed chair in the centre of the tent. By his side stood the two Lamas who had first entered with him. The Pombo was beyond doubt in a hypnotic trance. He sat motionless, with his hands flat on his knees and his head erect; his eyes were fixed and staring. He remained like this for some minutes. All the soldiers and people who had collected in front of the tent went down on their knees, laid their caps on the ground, and muttered prayers. One of the two Lamas, a fellow with evident mesmeric powers, now laid his hand upon the shoulders of the Pombo, who gradually raised his arms with hands outstretched and remained, as if in a cataleptic state, for a long time without moving.

Next the Lama touched the Pombo's neck with his thumbs, and caused his head to begin a rapid circular movement from left to right.

Certain exorcisms were pronounced by the hypnotizer. The Pombo began most extraordinary snake-like contortions, moving and twisting his arms, head, body, and legs. He worked himself, or rather was worked, into a frenzy that lasted some time. The crowd of devotees drew nearer and nearer to him, praying fervently. There were deep sighs and cries of astonishment, even of terror, when the Pombo performed some of the more eccentric movements with his limbs. Now and then this weird dance terminated in a strange posture, the Pombo actually doubling himself up with his head between his feet and his long, flat hat resting on the ground. While he was in this position, the bystanders went one by one to touch his feet and make low prostrations and salutations. At last the hypnotizer, seizing the Pombo's head between his hands, stared in his eyes, rubbed his forehead, and woke him from the trance. The Pombo was pale and exhausted. When he lay back on the chair his hat fell off. His clean-shaven head unmistakably showed that he, too, was a Lama. Indeed, he belonged to a very high order, probably the first rank after the Dalai Lama of Lhassa.

Katas were distributed after this performance to all the Tibetans present, who folded them and stowed them away in their coats.

The Pombo came out of his gaudy tent. I told him that the dance was beautiful, but I was very hungry. He asked me what I wanted to eat. I said I should like some meat and tea.

A little later a large vessel with a delicious stew of yak meat was brought to me, as well as *tsamba* in abundance. I felt famished, but I had the greatest difficulty in swallowing even a little food. This, I thought, must be owing to the injuries to my spine and the semi-mortification of my limbs, which had apparently affected my whole system except my head.

When the Pombo had retired and night came on, I was again tied to the stretching log. This time with my legs stretched not so far apart. My arms were again fastened to the pillar behind, but with no strain on them.

Late in the evening half a dozen Lamas came from the monastery with a light and a large brass bowl which, they said, contained tea. The wounded Lama, with his head bandaged up, was among them. He was so anxious for me to drink some of the steaming beverage, in order that I should keep warm during the cold night, that I became suspicious. When they pushed a bowl of the liquid to my lips, I merely sipped a little and declined to take more, spitting out what little they had poured into my mouth. I unfortunately swallowed a few drops. A few minutes later I was seized with sharp pains in my stomach, which continued for several days after. The drink proffered me was poisoned.

The following day my left foot, which had remained lifeless since I had been untied from the rack the first time, began to get better, and the circulation was gradually restored. The pain was unbearable.

In the morning indecision again prevailed as to what they would do to us. A number of Lamas were still anxious to have us beheaded, whereas the Pombo and the others had the previous night almost made up their minds to send us back to the frontier. Unluckily, it appears that the Pombo had a vision during the night. A spirit told him that, if he did not kill us, he and his country would suffer from a great calamity. "You can kill the *Plenki*," the spirit was reported to have said, "and no one will punish you if you do. The *Plenkis* are afraid to fight the Tibetans."

Among the Lamas no important step is taken without incantations and reference to occult science. The Pombo ordered a Lama to cut off a lock of my hair. A soldier did this with a blunt knife, and the Pombo rode up with it in his hands to the Lamasery to consult the oracle. The lock was handed in for examination. After certain incantations, the oracle answered that I must be beheaded or the country would be in great danger.

The Pombo rode back disappointed, and now ordered that one of my toe-nails should be cut. This operation was performed with the same blunt knife; the oracle was again consulted; the same answer was received.

Three such consultations are usually held by the high court of the assembled Lamas, the Tibetans on the third occasion producing for the oracle's decision a piece wrenched from a finger-nail. The Lama who performed this last operation examined my hands and spread my fingers apart, expressing intense astonishment. In a moment all the Lamas and soldiers came round and examined my hands—a repetition of my experience at the Tucker monastery. The Pombo, too, on being informed, immediately came and inspected my fingers. Matters from that moment took a different turn.

When, some weeks later, I was released I was able to learn from the Tibetans the reason of their amazement. My fingers happen to be webbed rather higher than usual. This is most highly thought of in Tibet. A person possessing such fingers has, according to the Tibetans, a charmed life. No matter how much is tried, no real harm can be done to him. Apart from the question whether there was much charm or not in my life in Tibet, there is no doubt that this trifling superstition did much toward hastening the Pombo's decision as to what was to be our fate.

The Pombo ordered that my life should be spared, and that I should on that very day start on my return journey toward the Indian frontier. He took from my own money one hundred and twenty rupees, which he placed in my pocket for my wants during the journey, and commanded that, though I must be kept chained up, I was to be treated kindly, and my servants also.

CHAPTER XXIII

LED TO THE FRONTIER

WHEN all was ready, Mansing and I were led on foot to Toxem. Our guard consisted of some fifty horsemen. We had to travel at a great speed despite our severely lacerated feet, our aching bones, and the sores and wounds with which we were covered all over. The soldiers led me tied by the neck like a dog, and dragged me along when, panting, exhausted, and suffering, I could not keep up with the ponies. We crossed several cold streams, sinking in water and mud up to our waists.

At Toxem, to my delight, I beheld Chanden Sing still alive. He had been kept prisoner in the mud house, where he had remained tied upright to a post for over three days. For four days he had eaten no food nor drunk anything. He was told that I had been beheaded. He was in a dreadful condition — almost dying from his wounds, cold, and starvation.

We were detained for the night in one of the rooms of the mud house. The place was packed with soldiers who gambled the whole night, and sang and swore and fought, preventing us from sleeping for even a few minutes. Wo were half choked by the smoke from the fire.

The next day at sunrise Chanden Sing and I were placed on yaks, not on riding-saddles, but on wooden pack-saddles. Poor Mansing was made to walk, and was beaten mercilessly when, tired and worn, he fell or remained behind. Finally they tied a rope round his neck and dragged him along in a most brutal manner. A strong guard prevented our escaping. The soldiers demanded fresh relays of yaks and ponies, and food for themselves, at all the encampments, so that we travelled fast. In the first five days we covered one hundred and seventy-eight miles, the two longest marches being, respectively, forty-two and forty-five miles. Afterward we did not march quite so quickly.

We suffered considerably on these long marches. The soldiers ill-treated us, and would not allow us to eat every day for fear we should get too strong. They let us have food only every two or three days. Our exhaustion and the pain caused by riding those wretched yaks in our wounded condition were terrible.

All our property had been taken away from us. Our clothes, in rags, were swarming with vermin. We were barefooted and almost naked. The first few days we generally marched from before sunrise till an hour or two after sunset. As soon as we reached camp we were torn off our yaks, and our jailers fastened heavy rings round our ankles, in addition to those we already had round our wrists. Thus hampered with chains, the Tibetans knew we could not possibly escape. We were left to sleep out in the open without a covering of any kind. Some nights we were lying on snow; other nights we were drenched in rain. Our guard generally pitched a tent under which they slept. Even when they did not have a shelter, they usually went to brew their tea some fifty yards or so from us.

Helped by my two servants, who sat by me to keep watch and to screen me, I managed, at considerable risk, to keep a rough record of the return journey, on a small piece of paper that had remained in my pocket when I had been searched by the Tibetans. My hands being supple, I was able to draw my right hand out of its cuff. Using as a pen a small piece of bone I had picked up, and my blood as ink, I drew brief cipher notes and a rough map of the entire route back.

Necessarily I had to content myself with taking my bearings by the sun, the position of which I got fairly accurately by constantly watching the shadow projected by my body on the ground. Of course, when it rained or snowed, I had to reckon my bearings by the observations of the previous day. We travelled first west, then successively west-north-west, north-west, west, and north-west, following the Brahmaputra along a course south of the outward journey, until we reached the boundary of the Yutzang (the Lhassa) province. The soldiers of our guard were severe with us. They ill-treated us in every possible way. Only one or two of the soldiers showed thoughtfulness, bringing us a little butter or *tsamba* whenever they could do so unseen by their comrades. The guard was changed so frequently that we had no chance of making friends with the men. Each lot seemed worse than the last.

A curious incident happened one day, causing a scare among the Tibetans. We had halted near a cliff. The soldiers were some twenty yards off. Having exhausted all other means to inspire these ruffians with respect, as a last resort I tried ventriloquism. I spoke, and pretended to receive answers to my words from the summit of the cliff. The Tibetans were terror-stricken. They asked me who was up there. I said it was some one I knew.

"Is it a *Plenki?*"

"Yes."

Immediately they hustled us on our yaks while they mounted their ponies, and we left the place at a great speed.

On reaching a spot, which from observations taken on my outward journey I reckoned to be in longitude 83° 6′ 30″ east, and latitude 30° 27′ 30″ north, I had a great piece of luck. It was at this point that the two principal sources of the Brahmaputra met and formed one river, one coming from the north-west, which I had already followed, the other coming from the west-north-west. The Tibetans, to my delight, selected the southern route, thus giving me an opportunity of visiting the second of the two principal sources of the great river. This second stream rose in a flat plain, having its first birth in a lakelet in approximate longitude 82° 47′ east and latitude 30° 33′ north. I gave the northern source my own name. I was glad to be the first white man to visit both sources of the Brahmaputra River.

Dreary as this period of captivity was, yet it was instructive. As we went along, I got the soldiers to teach me several Tibetan songs, and from the less ill-natured men of our guard I picked up, by judicious questioning, a considerable amount of information.

Over a more southerly and lower pass than the Maium Pass, by which, healthy, hopeful, and free, we had entered the province of Yutzang, we now left it, wounded, broken down, almost naked, and prisoners.

We proceeded in a north-westerly direction. Once clear of the sacred Yutzang province, our guard behaved with rather less cruelty. With the little money the Pombo had permitted me to keep we were now allowed to purchase food enough to provide us with more frequent meals. While we ate, the soldiers removed our handcuffs, which they temporarily placed round our ankles. With utensils lent us by our guard, we were able to cook some food. It seemed delicious. We used flat stones for dishes.

We crossed our former track, and then followed it almost in a parallel line, some miles north of it, along an undulating, clayey plateau, thus avoiding the marshy plain which we had found so troublesome to cross on our outward journey. We found a great number of black tents scattered here and there. One night, when encamped near some small lakes, we were allowed to purchase a goat. A soldier who had been friendly to us selected a fat one for us, and we were looking forward with pleasure to a solid meal when we found, to our dismay, that we had no means of dispatching the animal. We could not behead it, as the Tibetans would not trust us with a knife or sword. The Tibetans refused to kill the animal for us. Eventually our soldier friend allowed his scruples to be overcome by the payment of a rupee. He tied the animal's legs together, and having stopped up its nostrils with mud, he held the poor beast's mouth tightly with one hand until it died by suffocation. With his free hand the soldier during the performance revolved his prayer-wheel, praying fervently all the while.

We found ourselves at last in the plain, where a Tarjum's encampment of some two hundred tents was to be seen. Here we remained one night. There was a large assemblage of Lamas and soldiers. In the middle of the night we were roughly roused from our sleep, and made to move our camp about a mile or so from the settlement. Early in the morning, having crossed the large stream, we proceeded in a south-westerly direction, reaching the encampment of the Tokchim Tarjum the same night. Here we were met by the officers who had on a previous occasion, during our outward journey, brought us gifts, and whom we had routed with their soldiers when they had threatened us.

This time they behaved considerately. The oldest of them showed us great civility, and professed admiration for our perseverance against such heavy odds. The old gentleman did all he could to make us comfortable, and even got two strolling musicians to amuse us.

The next day, amid repeated good-byes and professions of friendship on the part of our hosts and jailers, we departed toward Mansarowar. Late in the afternoon we reached Tucker Village and Gomba, where we put up at the same *serai* in which we had slept on our way out. All our bonds were here removed, and we enjoyed comparative freedom, though four men walked by my side wherever I went, and an equal number looked after Chanden Sing and Mansing. Naturally we were not allowed to go far from the *serai*, but we could stroll about in the village. I took this opportunity to have a swim in the Mansarowar Lake. Chanden Sing and Mansing again paid fresh salaams to the gods, and also plunged into the sacred waters.

The local Lamas, who had been friendly during my former visit, were now extremely sulky and rude. Having witnessed our arrival, they withdrew into the monastery, slamming the gate after them. All the villagers, too, hastily retired to their respective houses. The place looked deserted with the exception of the soldiers round us.

Poor Mansing, who, worn out and in great pain, was sitting close by me, looking vaguely at the lake, had an extraordinary vision, the result, probably, of fever or exhaustion.

"Oh, sir," said he, as if in a dream, though he was quite awake, "look, look! Look at the crowd of people walking on the water! There must be more than a thousand men! Oh, how big they are getting! . . . And there is God! . . . No; they are Tibetans; they are coming to kill us; they are Lamas! Oh, come, sahib, they are near! . . . Oh, they are flying! . . ."

"Where are they?" I asked.

"They have all disappeared!" he exclaimed, as I placed my hand on his forehead and he woke from his trance.

I could see that the poor fellow was under an hallucination. His forehead was burning, and he had a high fever.

He seemed quite stupefied for a few moments. On my inquiring of him later whether he had seen the phantom crowd again, he could not remember ever having seen it at all.

The natives came to visit us in the *serai* during the evening. We had great fun with them. The Tibetans were full of humor and had comical ways. Now that we were only two marches from Taklakot, it was but natural that our spirits were high. Only two more days of captivity, and then a prospect of freedom!

It was still dark when we were roused and ordered to start. The soldiers dragged us out of the *serai*. We entreated them to let us have another plunge in the sacred Mansarowar, and the three of us were eventually allowed to do so. The water was bitterly cold, and we had nothing to dry ourselves with.

It was about an hour before sunrise when we were placed on our yaks and, surrounded by some thirty soldiers, rode off.

When we had been marching for several hours our guard halted to have their tea. A trader named Suna, and his brother and son, whom I had met in Garbyang, halted near us. From them I heard that news had arrived in India that my two men and I had been beheaded, and that thereupon Doctor Wilson and the British Political Officer, Karak Sing, had crossed over the frontier to ascertain the facts, and to attempt to recover my baggage, etc. My joy was intense when I heard that they were still at Taklakot. I persuaded Suna to return as fast as he could to inform Wilson that I was a prisoner, and to tell him my whereabouts. I had barely given Suna this message when our guard seized the man and his brother and roughly dismissed them, preventing them from having any further communication with us.

As soon as we were on the march again, a horseman rode up to us with strict orders from the Jong Pen of Taklakot not to let us proceed any farther toward the frontier by the Lippu Pass, which we could now have reached in two days, but to take us instead by the distant Lumpiya Pass. At that time of the year the Lumpiya would be impassable. We should have to make a further journey of at least fifteen or sixteen days, most of it over snow and ice, during which we, in our starved and weakened state, would inevitably die. We asked to be taken into Taklakot, but our guard refused. The Jong Pen of Taklakot had sent other messengers and soldiers to insure the fulfilment of his orders, and to prevent our further progress.

Our guard, now strengthened by the Taklakot men, compelled us to leave the Taklakot track, and we began our journey toward the cold Lumpiya. This was murder. The Tibetans, well knowing it, calculated on telling the British authorities that we had died of a natural death on the snows.

We were informed that we should be left at the point where the perpetual snows began, that the Tibetans would give us no food, no clothes and no blankets, and that we should be abandoned to cross over the frontier as best we could. This, needless to say, meant sure death.

After travelling some two and a half miles westward of the Taklakot track we declined to proceed any farther in that direction. We said that, if they attempted to compel us, we were prepared to fight our guard. Whether we died by their swords and matchlocks, or froze to death on the Lumpiya, was quite immaterial to us.

The guard, perplexed, decided to let us halt there for the night, so as to have time to send a messenger to Taklakot to inform the Jong Pen, and ask for further instructions.

During the night the order came that we must proceed, so the next morning our guard prepared to start us again toward the Lumpiya. It was at that moment that we three semi-corpses collected what little strength remained in us, and suddenly, with what stones we could pick up, made an attack on the soldiers. Incredible as it may seem, our cowardly guard bolted! We went on in the direction of Taklakot, followed at a distance by these ruffians, who were entreating us to make no further resistance and to go with them where they wanted us to go. If we did not, they said, they would all have their heads cut off. We refused to listen, and kept them away by throwing stones at them.

We had gone but a few miles when we met with a large force of soldiers and Lamas, dispatched by the Jong Pen to prepare for our death. Unarmed, wounded, starved, and exhausted as we were, it was useless attempting to fight against such odds. As it was, when they

WE ATTACKED OUR GUARD WITH STONES

saw we had regained our freedom, they made ready to fire on us.

The Jong Pen's chief minister, a man called Lapsang, and the Jong Pen's private secretary, were at the head of this party. I went to shake hands with them. A long and stormy palaver followed, but they kept firm and insisted on our turning away from the frontier, now that we were within a short distance of it. We must perforce proceed by the high Lumpiya Pass. Those were the Jong Pen's orders, and they, as well as I, must obey them. They would not give us or sell us either animals or clothes, which even the small sum of money I had on me would have been sufficient to buy. They would not provide us with an ounce of food. We emphatically protested, and said we preferred to die where we were. We asked them to kill us there and then, for we would not budge an inch westward.

Lapsang and the Jong Pen's private secretary now cunningly suggested that I should give them in writing the names of the Shokas who had accompanied me to Tibet. probably with the object of confiscating the land and goods of these former followers of mine. As I said I could not write Tibetan or Hindustani, they requested me to do it in English. This I did, but substituting for the names of my men and my signature sarcastic words, which must have caused the Tibetans surprise when they had the document translated.

The Tibetans refused to kill us there and then. Lapsang showed us great politeness, and asked us as a personal favor to him to go by the Lumpiya Pass. As I had no alternative I reluctantly decided to accept their terms rather than waste any more time talking.

Escorted by the large force of soldiers, we had nearly reached Kardam when a horseman came up at a full gallop and hailed our party. We stopped. The messenger overtook us and handed Lapsang a letter. It contained an order to bring us immediately into Taklakot.

We retraced our steps along the undulating plateau above the Gakkon River. Late at night we reached the village of Dogmar, a peculiar settlement in a valley between two high cliffs of clay. The natives lived in holes and chambers hollowed in the cliff.

Lapsang, the Jong Pen's private secretary, and the greater portion of the soldiers, having changed their ponies, went on to Taklakot. We were made to halt. Another letter came from the Jong Pen saying he had changed his mind, and we must, after all, go by the Lumpiya Pass!

CHAPTER XXIV

WITH FRIENDS AT LAST

In the night a large number of horsemen arrived. There was a great commotion in the place, the people running about shouting.

Tibet is farmed out to officials who have practically become small feudal kings, and who are constantly quarrelling with one another.

To royal jealousy, and to disputes over the rights of the road, was due the appearance of the new army. There were altogether some hundred and fifty men armed with matchlocks and swords. The chieftain of this band came to me with eight or ten other officers. He spoke so excitedly that I feared there was trouble in store for us. There was indeed. These new arrivals were officers and soldiers from the districts of Gyanema, Kardam, and Barca. They had come with strict orders from the Barca Tarjum that we were on no account to traverse his province or to cross into India by the Lumpiya Pass. This was both amusing and tantalizing, for we had now no way across the frontier open to us. Our guard and some of the Jong Pen's men who had remained behind, finding they were in the minority, thought it prudent to disappear. Anxious as I naturally was to get out of the country as quickly as possible, I approved of all the Gyanema men said, and urged them to fight in case the Jong Pen insisted on my going through the Tarjum's province. All ways out of the country were now barred to us, and unless we resorted to force, I felt we would never escape at all.

The Gyanema men asked me whether I would lead them in case of a fight with the Jong Pen's soldiers. Though not overconfident in their courage, I accepted the post of general-in-chief *pro tem.*, Chanden Sing and Mansing being elected there and then as my aides-de-camp. We spent the greater part of the night in arranging our plan of attack on the Jong Pen's troops. When all was properly settled, the Tibetans, to show their gratitude, brought me a leg of mutton, some *tsamba*, and two bricks of tea.

Morning came. I was given a beautiful pony to ride. Chanden Sing and Mansing were mounted on equally handsome animals. Then followed my Tibetan troops—a grand cavalcade. We started gayly toward Taklakot. We had been informed that the Jong Pen was concentrating his men at a certain point on the road, where he intended to bar our way. It was this point that we must force. My Tibetans said that they hated the Jong Pen's men, and swore they would slaughter them all if they dared to stand before us and prevent our passage.

"But they are such cowards." declared one of the Tibetan officers, "they will run away."

All this talk suddenly stopped when we heard the distant tinkling of our enemies' horse-bells. I encouraged my men as best I could, but a panic began to spread among them. The Jong Pen's men came in sight. I witnessed the strange spectacle of two armies face to face, each in mortal terror of the other.

Notwithstanding my remonstrances, matchlocks and swords were deposited on the ground with anxious eagerness by both parties, in order to show that only peaceful intentions prevailed. Then a conference was held, in which everybody seemed ready to oblige everybody else except me.

While this was still proceeding, a horseman arrived with a message from the Jong Pen, and at last, to everybody's satisfaction, permission was granted for us to proceed into Taklakot.

My army retraced its steps toward the north-west. Deposed from the high military post, which I had occupied only for a few hours, I became again a private individual and a prisoner. A large escort took us along a rocky road following the course of the Gakkon River along barren cliffs. We passed hundreds of *choktens*, large and small, mostly painted red, and *mani* walls. Then, having descended by a precipitous track on whitish clay-soil, we reached a thickly inhabited district, where stone houses were scattered all over the landscape. We saw on our left the large monastery of Delaling, and, a little way off, the Gomba of Sibling. Describing a sweeping curve among rocks and bowlders, we rounded the high, graceful cliff, on the top of which towered the fort and monasteries of Taklakot.

Such was our anxiety, when we reached this point, lest something should happen and we should be taken back again by another route, that as soon as we were across the wooden bridge over the Gakkon River, Chanden Sing and I, on perceiving the large Shoka encampment at the foot of the hill, lashed our ponies and ran away from our guard. Galloping our hardest along the high cliff, riddled with holes and passages in which the natives live, we found ourselves at last among friends again. The Shokas, who had come over to this market to exchange their goods with the Tibetans, were astounded when they saw us. They recognized us with great difficulty.

We inquired at once for Doctor Wilson. When we found him the good man could hardly recognize us, so changed were we. He seemed deeply moved at our pitiable condition.

When the news of our arrival spread in camp, we met with the greatest kindness at the hands of everybody. In a corner of Wilson's tent was a large quantity of candied sugar—several pounds. So famished was I that I threw myself on it and quickly devoured the lot. Later, my Shoka friends brought in all kinds of presents in the shape of eatables, and Rubso, the doctor's cook, was set to prepare an elaborate meal.

The British Political Frontier Officer, Karak Sing, hurried to me with a change of clothes. Other garments were given me by Doctor Wilson. My own ragged attire was literally swarming with vermin. Our guard had not allowed us a single change of clothes, nor would they even hear of our washing daily. It was by a special favor, and merely on account of its sanctity, that we were allowed to plunge into the sacred Mansarowar Lake.

Later in the day my wounds and injuries were examined by Doctor Wilson, who sent official reports to the Government of India.

Tenderly nursed by Wilson and Karak Sing, and having partaken of plenty of good food, my spirits, which had fallen rather low, revived as by magic. After a few hours of happiness, I was already beginning to forget the hardships and sufferings I had endured. I remained three days at Taklakot, during which time part of my confiscated baggage was returned to me by the Tibetans. I was overjoyed to discover that among the things thus recovered were my diary, note-books, maps, and sketches. My firearms, most of my money, the gold ring credited with wonderful powers, several mathematical instruments, collections, over four hundred photographic negatives, and various other articles were still missing,[1] but I was glad to get back as much as I did.

To Doctor Wilson's tent came the Tokchim Tarjum, his private secretary, Nerba, whom the reader may remember as having played an important part in my tortures, the Jong Pen's secretary, and Lapsang in his handsome green velvet coat with ample sleeves. These Tibetan officials admitted before the Political Officer, Doctor Wilson, Pundit Gobaria, and many Shokas, and even professed to be proud of what they had done to me. They used expressions not at all flattering to the British Government, for which they seemed to entertain great contempt.

I nearly got the Political Officer and the doctor into a

[1] Some of the articles missing were some months later recovered by the Government of India.

scrape. My blood, the little I had left, was boiling with rage at hearing the Tibetan insults. The climax came when Nerba refused to give back my mother's ring, which he had upon him. In a passion I seized a knife that was lying by me, and leaped upon Nerba, the ruffian who had once fired at me, and had held me by the hair while my eyes were being injured, as well as during the preliminaries for my execution. Wilson and Karak Sing checked me, and took the knife out of my hand. There was a general stampede of the Tibetan officers, and our interview and negotiations were brought to an abrupt end.

In further conversation I learned how my release had been brought about. Doctor Wilson and the Political Agent, having received news that my servants and myself had been beheaded, proceeded across the frontier to make inquiries and to try to recover my property. They heard only on arrival at Taklakot from the man Suna, whom I had sent from Mansarowar with my message, that I was still alive and a prisoner, covered with wounds, in rags, and starving. They had not enough men to force their way farther into the country to come and meet me. Besides, the Tibetans watched them carefully. Together with the influential Pundit Gobaria they made strong representations to the Jong Pen of Taklakot. By threatening him that an army would be sent to my rescue if I were not set at liberty, they at last obtained from the reluctant Tibetan potentate permission that I should be brought into Taklakot. The permission was afterward withdrawn, but was at last allowed to be carried into

CLIFF HABITATIONS

execution. It was entirely due to the good offices and energy of these three men that I was brought back alive.

Pundit Gobaria was the most influential Shoka chief and trader on our frontier in Bhot. He was on very friendly terms with the Tibetans and was the intermediary through whom negotiations were carried on for my immediate release. It was largely owing to his advice to the Jong Pen that the negotiations led to satisfactory results.

After a short rest to recover sufficient strength, I recommenced my journey toward India. Having crossed the Lippu Pass (16,780 feet) I found myself at last on British soil again. We descended by slow stages to Gungi, where, in Doctor Wilson's dispensary, I had to halt for a few days on account of my weak condition.

Wilson had here a quantity of my baggage, instruments, cameras, plates, etc., which I had discarded at the beginning of my journey. They came handy. I had photographs taken of my two servants and myself, showing our wounds and general condition. In the full-face photograph, reproduced in this book, can be noticed the injuries to my left eye, as well as the marks of the hot-iron torture on the skin of my forehead and nose. I could see comparatively well with my right eye, but was unable to use the left eye at all.

The injuries to my spine were severe, and gave me much trouble. At times the whole of my left side became as if paralyzed. I experienced great difficulty in sitting down when I had been standing, and in getting up when I had been sitting down. Through the great strain they had undergone, my joints were stiff and swollen, and remained so for several months.

I was anxious to return to Europe as soon as possible. From Gungi and Garbyang I travelled down to Askote in the company of the Political Agent. The Nerpani road had fallen in two or three places. Rough, shaky bridges had been constructed across the deep precipices. We met with a hearty reception everywhere, and kindness was showered upon us by all alike.

At Askote I met Mr. J. Larkin, hastily dispatched by the Government of India to the frontier to conduct an inquiry into my case. Though still suffering much pain, I insisted on turning back once more toward Tibet to help him in his task. By quick marches we reached Garbyang and climbed toward the snows. We intended crossing over the Lippu Pass into Tibet to give the Jong Pen an opportunity of being interviewed. The Tibetan official refused to meet us.

In order to give the Tibetans every chance, we climbed over the Lippu Pass. It had been snowing heavily, and it was very cold. A Shoka had only a few days previously been frozen to death in the snow trying to cross over the pass. There were some twelve feet of snow, and the ascent was not easy. Toiling for two hours from our last camp on the mountain-side, we reached the summit of the pass. I was once more in Tibet. Doctor Wilson, the Political Agent, and others were with us. Having found a suitable spot where the wind did not cut quite so furiously into our faces, we halted for a considerable time and waited impatiently on the Tibetan side of the boundary for the

Jong Pen or his deputies, to whom letters had been sent asking them to come and meet us. They did not put in an appearance.

In the afternoon of October 12th I finally turned my back on the Forbidden Land. I was still far from well, but was glad indeed at the prospect of seeing England and my friends again.

We returned to our camp, a few hundred feet lower than the pass, where we had left our baggage and many of our men who were laid up with mountain sickness.

Having fulfilled our mission, Mr. Larkin and I returned by quick marches to Almora. In conducting the inquiry for the British Government, Mr. Larkin obtained at the frontier ample testimony of what had occurred. A full report was sent to the Government of India, and to the Foreign Office and India Office in London. A copy of the Government Report will be found in the Appendix.

Winter setting in, the Shokas, who had then all returned from Tibet, were beginning to migrate to their winter homes lower down on the mountains. When we passed the settlement many were already at work repairing the fallen-down roofs of their winter habitations. A large number of Tibetans with their sheep had also come over to spend the winter on British territory. Their encampments could be seen all along the road wherever there was sufficient grass for their flocks. The Tibetans—Lamas and officials—maintained a high-handed and insolent demeanor as long as we were in Bhot, which they regarded as part of their own country, but which was in reality British soil. It must, however, be said for them that the moment they came out of Bhot, and had to deal with Hindoos instead of Shokas, their manner changed considerably. Servility took the place of haughtiness and insolence.

We proceeded with no delay to Almora, and from there to Naini Tal, the summer seat of the Government of the North-West Provinces and Oudh. At the latter place a conference was held on my case by the Lieutenant-Governor.

I paid off my faithful coolie Mansing, giving him enough for a start in life. He accompanied me to Kathgodam, the northern terminus of the railway. Genuine grief showed on his face when Chanden Sing and I stepped into the train. He begged that, if ever I should go back to Tibet, I must take him with me; only next time he, too, must be provided with a rifle! That was the only condition. As the train steamed away from the platform, he waved his hand affectionately.

Chanden Sing, who remained as my servant, travelled with me to Bombay, and from there we went direct to Florence, the home of my parents, who had suffered in their anxiety at home almost as much as I did in the Forbidden Land.

APPENDIX

Letter from Sir William Lee Warner, C.S.I., *Political and Secret Department, India Office, London.*

India Office, Whitehall, S.W.
August 4, 1898.

Dear Sir,

With reference to the request contained in your letter of the 27th, and to your interview with me of the same day, I forward herewith for your use a copy of Mr. Larkin's "Inquiry and report" into your treatment by the Tibetans.

Yours faithfully,
(Signed) W. Lee Warner.

A. Henry Savage Landor, Esq.

GOVERNMENT REPORT BY J. LARKIN, Esq., MAGISTRATE OF THE FIRST CLASS

Mr. Arnold Henry Savage Landor having been reported to have been captured and tortured by the Tibetans, I was sent up to Garbyang in Byans to ascertain the facts.

Mr. Landor arrived in India on the 10th of April last. He proceeded to Almora, where he arrived on the 27th idem. He stayed there until the 10th of May, to make arrangements for his travels in Tibet. At first he was advised to take some Gurkha soldiers with him, but this fell through, as the military did not accede to his request. He then, on the 27th May, arrived in Garbyang in Byans *patti*. It appears to have been his intention to have entered Tibet by the Lippu Lek Pass. This is the easiest, being about 16,780 feet above sea-level. It is the most frequented route taken by the traders of Byans and Chaudans, and is adjacent to Taklakot, a mart for wool, salt, borax, grain, etc. He was, however, frustrated in this, inasmuch as the Jong Pen of Taklakot came to know of Mr. Landor's intention and took steps to prevent it. He caused bridges to be destroyed and stationed guards along the route.

Moreover, he appears to have been kept fully cognizant of Mr. Landor's moves through the agency of his spies in Garbyang.

Under these circumstances Mr. Landor was compelled to resort to some other route, and selected the Lumpia Pass, which stands at an altitude of 18,150 feet.

On the 13th July last Mr. Landor, with a following of thirty men, entered Tibet. He reached Gyanima, where he was stopped by the Barkha Tarjum. This personage, however, after some persuasion, consented to permit Mr. Landor and seven followers to go forward to the Mansarowar Lake.

Next day the accorded permission was withdrawn, and Mr. Landor and his party were turned back. The party returned three marches, when Mr. Savage Landor determined to go to Mansarowar by the unfrequented wilds.

On the 21st July Mr. Landor, with nine followers, at midnight, in a terrific snow-storm, climbed up the mountain and went off, the bulk of his party continuing their retreat to the Lumpia Lek. By this strategic move Mr. Landor baffled the Tibetan guards (*Chaukìdárs*). He carefully avoided coming into contact with any of the inhabitants, and in order to do so was obliged to keep to the high mountains and unfrequented wilds.

Travelling thus, with the aid of his compass, sextant, and sketch maps, he reached Mansarowar.

Here five of his followers declined to accompany him any farther, so he paid and dismissed them. This was at Tucker. Thus Mr. Landor was reduced to a following of four men. He went on, however, and had accomplished but three marches more when two more of his followers deserted him at night. These went off with some of his supplies, all his servants' food, and ropes.

Mr. Landor was now reduced to the following of a bearer (Chanden Sing) and a coolie (Mansing). Despite his misfortunes he determined to push on: his intention appears to have been to reach Lhassa.

He went over the Mariam La Pass.[1] This attains an altitude of over 16,000 feet.

Meanwhile the deserters had bruited about the information of Mr. Landor's intention of getting to Lhassa.

While crossing the Neo (Tsambo) River one of Mr. Landor's yaks went under. The yak was saved, but its valuable load, consisting of all the tinned provisions, Rs. 800 in cash, three pairs of shoes, one slaughtered sheep, wearing apparel, razors, skinning instruments, and some three hundred rifle cartridges, was lost.

This accident was directly the cause of Mr. Landor's capture, as he and his two followers, who were footsore, starving, and disheartened, were driven to seek food and horses from the inhabitants of the country. On the 19th of August, 1897, they went to a place called Toxem. The villagers received them well and promised to supply them with food and horses. Next morning, the 20th idem, a number of Tibetans came to Mr. Landor's tent, bringing food and ponies.

While Mr. Landor and his servants were engaged trying and selecting ponies, the crowd increased and came up behind its three victims.

Suddenly, without any warning, the Tibetans rushed on Mr. Landor and his two servants, and, overwhelming them by numbers, made prisoners of them. They cruelly bound their surprised victims. Then a number of soldiers (who had lain in ambush) arrived and took over the prisoners. The first person to be dealt with was the bearer Chanden Sing. He was accused of having taken his master into Tibet. He was questioned as to this, and also as to the maps and sketches found with Mr. Lan-

[1] Maium Pass.

dor's things. I may mention that when the arrests were made the Tibetans took all of Mr. Landor's property, which they handled very roughly, damaging most of the things. Hearing the Tibetans accuse the bearer, Mr. Landor called out that his servant was in no way responsible for his having entered Tibet. Thereupon a Lama struck him (Mr. Landor) a blow on the head with the butt-end of his riding-whip. Chanden Sing was then tied down and flogged. He received two hundred lashes with whips, wielded by two Lamas. Then the prisoners were kept apart for the night, bound with cords. Next day Mr. Landor was placed on a horse, seated on a spiked pack-saddle. Mansing was put on a bare-backed horse. They still were bound. Mr. Landor's arms were secured behind his back. Thus they were taken off at a gallop toward Galshio. When the party were nearing that place they came up with a party of Lamas, awaiting them by the roadside. Here Mr. Landor's horse was whipped and urged to the front. A kneeling soldier, his musket resting on a prop, fired at Mr. Landor as he went past. The shot failed to take effect. Then they stopped the pony and fastened a long cord to Mr. Landor's handcuffs. The other end was held by a soldier on horseback. The party then continued their career, the Lamas having fallen in. While proceeding at full gallop, the horseman who held the cord attached to Mr. Landor's handcuffs pulled hard at it to try and unhorse the latter. Had this occurred Mr. Landor must have been trampled to death under the troop of horsemen behind him. Thus they hurried onward till they neared Galshio,[1] when at a turn in the road a soldier was seen kneeling at the "ready," who fired a shot at Mr. Landor as he came abreast of him. This, like the previous shot, missed its object.

Arriving at Galshio, Mr. Landor was torn off his pony. He was in a bleeding state, the spikes in the pack-saddle having severely wounded his back. He asked for a few minutes' respite, but was jeeringly told by his guards that it was superfluous, as

[1] Galshio, or Gyatsho.

he was to be beheaded in a few minutes. He was then taken, his legs stretched as far as they could be forced apart, and then tied to the sharp edge of a log shaped like a prism. The cords were bound so tightly that they cut into the flesh.

Then a person named Nerba, the secretary of the Tokchim Tarjum, seized Mr. Landor by the hair of his head, and the chief official, termed the *Pombo,* came up with a red-hot iron, which he placed in very close proximity to Mr. Landor's eyes. The heat was so intense that for some moments Mr. Landor felt as if his eyes had been scorched out. It had been placed so close that it burned his nose. The *Pombo* next took a matchlock, which he rested on his victim's forehead and then discharged upward.

The shock was consequently very much felt. Handing the empty gun to an attendant soldier, the *Pombo* took a two-handed sword. He laid the sharp edge on the side of his victim's neck as if to measure the distance to make a true blow. Then wielding the sword aloft, he made it whiz past Mr. Landor's neck. This he repeated on the other side of the neck.

After this tragic performance Mr. Landor was thrown to the ground and a cloth put over his head and face to prevent his seeing what was being done to his servant Mansing. This must have been done to make Mr. Landor believe that Mansing was being executed. After a short time the cloth was removed and Mr. Landor beheld his servant, with his legs stretched, tied to the same log. Mr. Landor was kept for twenty-four hours in this trying position, legs stretched as far as possible and arms bound to a pole, and Mansing for twelve hours. To add to their misery, they were kept in the rain and were afterward seated in a pool of water. The effect of this torture was to strain the muscles of the legs and arms and injure the spine.

When Mr. Landor's legs were unloosed from their cords, they were so numbed and swollen that for sixteen hours he did not recover the use of them and feared they were mortifying. Mr. Landor's property was overhauled by the officials of Galshio and sealed up. On the afternoon of the third day, at Galshio, the two prisoners were taken on foot to Toxem. It was a very trying march, inasmuch as several rivers had to be crossed.

On his arrival at Toxem, Mr. Landor saw his bearer Chanden Sing, in a very precarious condition, as the latter had had no food for four days. During all this time the prisoners were firmly bound and carefully guarded. Next day, Mr. Landor and Chanden Sing were placed on yaks. Mansing had to walk. Thus they were taken in the direction of Mansarowar Lake. It was only on arrival at Mansarowar that his guards unbound Mr. Landor.

Arriving at Dogmar, the party was stopped by the Jong Pen of Taklakot, who refused to give them passage through his district. This was a very serious affair, as it meant that the worn-out prisoners would have to be taken by a long, circuitous route *via* Gyanima and into India by the Lumpia Pass. This would probably have done for them. Owing to the intervention of the Rev. Harkua Wilson, of the Methodist Episcopal Mission, *Peshkâr* Kharak Sing Pal and Pundit Gobaria, the most influential person among the Bhutias [1] of Byans, the Jong Pen was compelled to withdraw his prohibition and give his sanction to the prisoners being conveyed to Taklakot.

Arriving at this place the prisoners were hospitably received by the Rev. Harkua Wilson, who is also a medical man. He examined their injuries and attended to them. His statement discloses the dreadful condition he found them in. The Tibetan guards made over some of Mr. Landor's property to him at Taklakot. It was then found that much property had not been restored. Mr. Landor had a list drawn up from memory of his unrestored property. This list (a copy) was handed to the Jong Pen of Taklakot.

I append the list. The Jong Pen has been called upon to restore the missing articles. He urges that the affair did not occur in his district, and that he is in no way responsible for the loss of the property.

[1] Bhutias, or Shokas.

He has, however, promised to try to recover them, alleging that the affair has been reported to a superior authority at Gartok. From what I could gather here, it seems probable that all the missing property, save the money, will be restored. I tried to see the Jong Pen, but he pleaded illness and the inutility of a meeting in which he had nothing new to disclose. This personage is notorious in these parts for his implacable hatred to English subjects.

The account of the affair as given by Mr. Savage Landor is fully borne out by his two servants, and, moreover, the Tibetans who took part in it did not try to hide it.

In the Rev. Harkua Wilson's tent at Taklakot, before *Peshkár* Kharak Sing, Pundit Gobaria, and a large number of Bhutias, several Tibetan officials corroborated the whole account as related by Mr. Landor. The man Nerba, who had held Mr. Landor's hair when about to be beheaded and have his eyes burned out, admitted he had taken such part in the affair. There can be no doubt that the above account is true and unexaggerated, for the whole of Byans and Chaudans are ringing with it. The Jong Pen of Taklakot was given ample opportunity to explain the affair, but he declined to do so.

Mr. Savage Landor held Chinese passports, and his conduct during his stay in that country did not warrant the officials to have treated him in the barbarous, cruel way they did. I satisfied myself, by careful inquiry from the people here, as to how Mr. Landor behaved.

He is said to have been most munificent in his dealings with all, and invariably affable and courteous. I had seen Mr. Landor just before his entry into Tibet, and when I met him I could scarcely recognize him, though he had then fairly recovered from the terrible treatment he had received. I saw the marks of the cords on his hands and feet, and they are still visible after this lapse of time. He complains that he is still suffering from the injury done to his spine, and fears that it may be of a permanent nature.

October 15, 1897. J. LARKIN.

All communications to Government should give the No., date, and subject of any previous correspondence, and should note the Department quoted.

645

No. N. 277 A. of 189—.

From

THE UNDER-SECRETARY TO GOVERNMENT, N.-W. Provinces and Oudh.

To

A. H. SAVAGE LANDOR, Esq.,
% Messrs. GRINDLAY, GROOM & Co.,
Bankers, Bombay.

Dated, ALLAHABAD, *November* 13, 1897.

Political Department.

SIR,

In reply to your letter of November 5, I am desired to send you a printed copy of depositions recorded by Mr. Larkin as noted below:

1. Of yourself; 2. Of Chanden Sing;
3. Of Man Sing; 4. Of Rev. Harkua Wilson;
5. Of Pundit Gobaria; 6. Of Kharak Sing;
7. Of Suna.

I have the honor to be, Sir,

Your most obedient Servant,

H. N. WRIGHT,

Under-Secretary to Government, North-Western Provinces and Oudh. N.M.

DEPOSITION OF CHANDEN SING, *taken on the 9th day of October,* 1897.

Solemn affirmation administered by me.

My name is Chanden Sing; my father's name is Bije Singh; I am by caste Thatola; thirty-two years of age; by occupation *kheti;* my home is at That, police station Bisot, district Almora.

I took service as a bearer with Mr. Landor at Almora on the 27th or 28th of April last. I accompanied him on his trip to Tibet. We went along through the wilds, encountering many hardships and reached Toxem. There I insisted on my master buying ponies to take us to Darjeeling. This resulted in our capture, for up to then we had vigilantly kept away from the people. The people who brought us ponies to buy played us false. They informed the authorities, who sent soldiers, who lay in ambush behind the sand-hills until the crowd of horse-dealers and lookers-on, whom we did not suspect of treachery, surrounded and seized us. We were bound with cords by the arms (at back) and legs. My master was more cruelly tied than we two servants. We were taken to the Raja,[1] who accused me of having brought my master into the country. I was then stretched out and two strong men with whips inflicted two hundred stripes on me. I was questioned as to the maps. My master called out that he, not I, alone understood them, and asked that I should not be beaten. Thereupon a Lama struck him across the head and removed him to a distance, so that I could not communicate with him. They took all our property. Then we were kept separate for the night. I was put in a room and my hands tied to a pole. I could not sleep with the pain I was in. Next day my master, with his hands tied behind his back, was put on a spiked saddle and tied by a long rope held by a horseman. He went at a gallop surrounded by about fifty horsemen armed with guns and swords. Man Sing, our coolie, was also taken with him. My guards informed me my master was to be decapitated at Galshio, and that I was to be beheaded where I was. On the fourth or fifth day my master returned. Meanwhile I was a close prisoner, bound up, without food. When I saw my master he was in a pitiful state. He was handcuffed with enormous cuffs, clothes torn to rags, bleeding from his waist, feet and hands swollen. Next day a guard on horseback took us back, bound as we were, on yaks' backs, toward Mansarowar. There I had my cords unloosed. My master was kept bound until we got to Tangchim. We were eventually taken to Taklakot, where the Rev. Harkua Wilson met us and saw our condition. He attended to our wants. My master was well-nigh at death's door. The Tibetans returned some of my master's property, but they have kept about 475 rupees in cash, two rifles, revolver, two files, a

[1] Raja, or King.

lot of soap, medicine, a butterfly dodger, matches, a box of mathematical instruments, a quantity (400) cartridges, a large box of photographic plates and negatives, three bags. We did not molest any one, and paid more than four times the value for any food we bought.

Read over to witness.

J. LARKIN.

N.B.—For numerous other depositions, documents, and certificates, see larger edition of *In the Forbidden Land*.

THE END